When I die I have one simple request . . .
Just carry my casket up Lansdowne Avenue
to the Upper Darby High School. I would like to be
accompanied by the fanfare of the Senior High's Marching Royals.
Take my remains into the Performing Arts Center. Then serenade my farewell
with a gala student concert. And I will have found peace and joy in a place that
I have loved amidst abundant memories of those whom I have loved. . . .

The Author

CONTENTS

Preface		vii
Prologue		ix
1	High School Reminiscences	1
2	Joey Goes to College	7
3	Disillusionment or Determination	13
4	The Political Factor	17
5	Wally Wonder	21
6	Getting Things Done!	25
7	Construction Nightmares Avoided	29
8	Ethical Considerations	33
9	Just a Few Thoughts on Teachers and Teaching	39
10	Special Projects	43
11	A Dose of New Thinking, Please!	47
12	What Communication?!	53

CONTENTS

13	Harrisburg Forever!	61
14	Just a Few Words about Upper Darby Students	65
15	Mother Teresa	71
16	My Ode to the Upper Darby School Community	75

Epilogue	79
A Summary of the Messages of This Book	83
Bibliography	87
About The Author	89

PREFACE

In large part, this book is about school leadership. Much of it focuses on the unusual tactics of a real-life superintendent of schools over a long period of time. This leader's ideas, strategies, and actions are all hanging out there in full view as is much of his private life.

What this leader thought and did is certainly open to discussion and debate. And that is as it should be, for there are no magical prescriptions for effective school leadership. Every school community with its unique characteristics and set of human dynamics offers different challenges. And since each leader manages with his or her very own style, philosophy, and motivational set—not some prescriptive textbook—the portraits of effective school leaders are elusive. That having been said, there is only one Joey, as you will soon find out when you enter the pages that follow.

Beyond the issues of school leadership, this book is also about the complexities of public education, its aspirations and ideals, the qualities of people who work inside those schools, and the propaganda and villains that surround them. As such, this is a book for anyone who cares about education in America.

PROLOGUE

It was springtime in Philadelphia. Sal, Rocco, and Joey were in eighth grade. In just two months, the three friends would put their unpleasant Catholic elementary school experience behind them forever. The three boys were fed up with the arbitrary and brutal behavior of their nun overseers. Besides that, Sal and Rocco had no interest in things academic. They were marginal students who were usually in trouble in and out of school. In the fall, Sal and Rocco would start attending the area Catholic high school with Joey. But Sal and Rocco had goals that were much different than Joey's. They had firm plans to drop out of school after their sophomore year at age sixteen, when they could be legally signed out by their parents. Sal and Rocco would then pursue money full-time on the streets in the illegal ways of their fathers.

In contrast, Joey had dreams of college, although no one in his family had ever gone down that road. He was a well-behaved, above-average student who thought he might actually enjoy school if he could just get away from the vicious nuns who had terrorized him for the last eight years. Joey looked forward to high school, where he had heard on good authority that the Christian Brothers only whacked you if you did something wrong. What a wonderful concept! Only two more months until liberation!

As did most boys their age, Sal, Rocco, and Joey engaged in many naive but titillating conversations about the opposite sex. However, Sal, in particular, was obsessed with just one lovely, blue-eyed classmate, Theresa. He talked about her constantly, and he was determined to take her to a movie.

PROLOGUE

Rocco and Joey were aghast at this idea. They argued with Sal that this was a death wish for him. That's because Sister Magdalena, Mother Superior of their school, had issued a clear and threatening prohibition against dating to all of the school's upper-grade pupils. Anyone violating Sister Magdalena's edict would ultimately burn in hell and, worse yet, answer to her directly!

Undaunted, Theresa and Sal went to the local movie theater to view the Roy Rogers/Flash Gordon double feature matinee on a Saturday afternoon in late April. They did many evil things like holding hands and sharing popcorn together. Sal then returned to the company of Rocco and Joey with a glow of manly pride. He had stars in his eyes and looked to be in a trance. Rocco and Joey were filled with trepidation. This love stuff could be dangerous. The nuns had spies everywhere—weakling students who traded neighborhood gossip with the sisters in return for favored treatment in the classroom. If Sister Magdalena got wind of Theresa and Sal having a date, there would be hell to pay!

Sure enough, on Monday afternoon, just two days after Sal had tempted the fates with Theresa, the eighth-grade class was taken en masse from the school and seated in the front pews of the parish church adjacent to the school. This signaled something serious. Sister Magdalena didn't waste any time. She stood directly in front of the main altar and summoned Theresa and Sal to join her. Theresa was a sinner. Sal was a bum. They were each purveyors of filth. Let the beatings begin!

Sister Magdalena backhanded Theresa with a forceful wallop to her face. Theresa crashed backward into the altar rail, blood flowing from her nose and mouth. Within a millisecond, the huge nun began choking Sal, squeezing the life out of him, shaking his head back and forth so that Sal's eyes bulged and his body staggered. The eighth-grade audience sat silent, stunned, and horrified. Sister Magdalena was now pummeling Sal with rapid-fire smacks to his face.

Joey and Rocco were seated in the third pew. Rocco cursed under his breath and then jumped up and stood on the pew, screaming directly at Sister Magdalena: "This ain't right. It ain't even Catholic. They didn't do nothin' wrong. God will make you pay for this!"

A terrified Joey knew better than to get involved, but, operating on adrenaline, he joined the battle and chimed in: "This is a violation of human rights. It's against the law. We'll get a lawyer. How can you be doing this in the sight of God?"

PROLOGUE

Sister Magdalena's face was bright crimson. "Heathen vermin scum. How dare you question me? Both of you get up here. You can join your friends in righteous punishment."

All hell now broke loose. Rocco and Joey sat tight, so the irate nun came after them. Released from the nun's clutches, Sal now ran for his life toward the back of the church and an exit. Sister Magdalena had two new objectives for destruction. But as she approached them, Rocco and Joey raced out of their pew and joined Sal on the lam. The three boys sprinted out the front doors of the church without looking back as the nun's threats echoed behind them.

The three friends eventually ended up at a small hobo camp aside the train tracks near the school. Given the circumstances, there was no sense going home. All of their parents thought that beatings of their kids by nuns were a good thing. And disrespect of a nun, which undoubtedly had been reported to their homes by now, would lead to more physical abuse from parents. There seemed to be no way out. Sal and Rocco advocated catching the next freight train to anywhere. Campfires were burning, and some friendly train hustlers gave the boys cups of homemade soup and a blanket to sit on. Nice hospitality. But police sirens were wailing in the distance, a reminder to the boys that their world was ending. The despondent boys sat silently around one of the campfires. Nightfall arrived. The boys weren't going anywhere. Joey needed time to think.

Sometime after midnight, Joey awakened Sal and Rocco. Joey hadn't slept a wink. He had been developing a plan. The scheme depended on the belief that there was only one way to control Sister Magdalena. Joey shared his scenario with his desperate friends. Sal and Rocco listened intently. Eventually, they all agreed Joey's strategy had a chance, the only one they had!

The next morning before the sun rose, Sal, Rocco, and Joey had departed the hobo camp and were hidden in the bushes outside the front entrance to the church from which they had fled the previous afternoon. They didn't have a long wait. Grigor, the parish custodian, stumbled sleepily toward the church doors at about 6:00 A.M. and unlocked the entrances, opening up for parishioners to attend the 7:00 A.M. daily mass. Just as soon as Grigor went elsewhere, Sal, Rocco, and Joey entered the church and seated themselves in the very front pew before the main altar where yesterday's chaos had ensued. It was time to carry out the plan.

PROLOGUE

At about 6:15 A.M., Father Claude, the pastor, arrived to get the altar ready for mass. The priest was astonished to find the three missing convicts with heads bowed, kneeling with folded hands in the front pew. Police and frantic parents had been searching everywhere for them. The curtain rose, and Joey gave the performance of his life. Lord have mercy! He had rehearsed his speech many times during the long night; Joey spoke slowly and emotionally: "Father, we know we did something terribly wrong. We can offer no excuses. We are heartily sorry for our sins. That's why we've been here in church praying for forgiveness and guidance the entire night. We've been having a special novena. We sneaked in last night just before Grigor locked up the church and we've had a very spiritual experience for many hours. We humbly ask for your absolution. Whatever happens next, we have come back to our church and we have found peace in our hearts and with God!"

Father Claude was visibly moved. The priest knew a miracle when he saw one. For Sal and Rocco to have been praying all night was a divine sign. He now understood why God had united Joey with two such corrupt friends—to save them. Father Claude sent for Sister Magdalena.

"The Lord works in strange ways," Father Claude told the Mother Superior with unquestioned authority. "And that is why you will forgive Sal and Rocco and try in a more gentle manner to save their souls before they leave us for high school in two months. For now, call their parents and tell them that the boys are safe and that they too should welcome their sons back with loving arms, for a holy miracle has occurred. As for Joey, I have always known that he was special. Joey is going to save many souls in his lifetime!"

And so it came to pass that the last two months of Catholic elementary school were days of peace and tranquility for the Three Musketeers. Joey's brainpower and persuasive oratory had saved the doomed trio from a disaster. Sister Magdalena was neutralized. Joey soon concluded that school wasn't really so bad when you weren't getting beaten and traumatized. He was ready for high school. Sal and Rocco stayed out of trouble for the remainder of the school year and were actually promoted to the ninth grade. At Joey's direction, his two friends were even polite and courteous to the hated Sister Magdalena, who only rolled her skeptical eyes when they addressed her. Sadly, at the direction of her parents, Theresa, who miraculously escaped any cosmetic damage to her face from Sister Magdalena's beating, never spoke to Sal, Rocco, or Joey again.

1

HIGH SCHOOL REMINISCENCES

There were about 2,000 boys in my new high school, a big and bustling and fearsome place, especially when you came from a small school in a tiny Catholic parish as I did. It was hard to believe that Sal and Rocco were in this same building with me each school day because I rarely saw my old buddies. That's because Sal and Rocco were tracked into some out-of-sight technical program for incorrigibles. God, was I lonely.

My new college preparatory classmates were strangers to me, almost entirely from the larger and more affluent Catholic parishes. The first thing I noticed in high school was a great many students wearing the hip collegiate attire of the day: tan or beige khakis topped by narrow, ivy league stripped ties and a variety of colored blazers or tweed sportcoats. The finishing touches were either two-tone white-and-black saddle shoes, tan suede bucks, or brown or black loafers. N.B. Sportcoats or suit jackets with ties were mandatory while attending classes!

Given the economic status of my family, I had no chance of dressing in this style. The money my maintenance-man father earned went for food and housing. There wasn't any budgetary provision for new clothes. And so I stood out like a sore thumb among my classmates. My outdated plaid sportcoat had been acquired by my mother from her funeral-director friend who had recycled a set of clothes from a dead body after the grieving family showed no interest. At least it fit!

I did own two worn white dress shirts, which I alternated every other day with either of my father's two out-of-style, wide flower-print ties. My shoes

CHAPTER 1

were badly scarred black leather with shoelaces (unfortunately not loafers). My two worn pairs of pants were blue and black, respectively (no khakis in my wardrobe). Let's just say, I was not your basic, well-dressed Joey College! Nevertheless, I was excited at starting high school and determined to succeed. Whoever said that clothes make the man? So a few of my classmates snickered and mocked my attire. I could handle it. So what!

About a month into my high school mission, as I tried to confront Latin and algebra and science, subjects I had never seen in elementary school, my life changed forever. And not for the better.

Being dressed formally going back and forth on public transit to school was anathema to my high school classmates. So almost every student placed his sportcoat and ties in his individual locker at the end of the school day and traveled home much more comfortably in shirt sleeves or with outercoats or school jackets as the weather required. In the morning, when pupils arrived for school, it was just a simple matter of opening the locker, inserting the outerwear (if any), putting on the tie and sportcoat that was inside, and heading off to class in compliance with school rules. I thought this was a great custom, especially since my sportcoat was something I was ashamed of anyway.

On a bright fall day sometime in October of my freshman year, I arrived at school the usual fifteen minutes early and went straight to my third-floor locker to get my tie and sportcoat. I should have immediately known something was wrong when almost all of the boys congregating around their lockers had ridiculous smiles on their faces. And then I saw it. My plaid sportcoat had been excruciatingly pulled through the seams around my metal locker door. It was shredded to pieces, partly from being yanked through the locker's cracks and more obviously from being cut up badly by some knife-wielding loonies. The hallway rocked with sarcastic laughter from the student onlookers. Initially, my heart had stopped beating when I saw the vandalism; now my heart began to bleed, and my eyes filled up with tears. I sank to my knees despairing in front of my locker. The warning bell sounded throughout the high school, indicating two minutes for pupils to get to homeroom. The hallway quickly emptied out. I just stayed there on the floor paralyzed with internal pain.

The late bell now shrilled, waking me from my coma. I didn't know what to do. Down the hall came the school disciplinarian, Brother Dennis, search-

HIGH SCHOOL REMINISCENCES

ing for tardy students. Nobody messed with Brother Dennis. He was big, bad, and no nonsense. I expected to die. But Brother Dennis was also no fool. He quickly appraised the situation and did what not one fellow student would do. He comforted me. Brother Dennis told me that he would find the perps who had destroyed my sportcoat and make them pay. For the present, I should get to my first-period class and tell the Brother teaching the class that Brother Dennis would show up in ten minutes or so to explain about my lack of a tie and sportcoat. I was uplifted. Someone actually cared about me. I began blinking rapidly to hide my tears and headed for class.

Cautiously, I entered my first-period English class already in session with Brother Ricardo. I stood politely in the doorway, waiting for a chance to offer my explanation. But before I could say a word, Brother Ricardo glared at me and then exploded: "What the hell is this? You dare come to class late, looking like a piece of trash. You're an insult to the human race."

I tried to get a word in, but Brother Ricardo was quick. He punched me in the right side of my face. I fell backward against the wall. Entertainment with a message for my classmates. I covered up defensively. He was going to hit me again. No way would I put up with any more of this. I lurched forward and thought about slugging my attacker. "Don't you dare touch me again," I screamed. "I've had it with this hell hole. I'm getting outta here." I ran out of the classroom and the high school and raced like a mad dog, dodging traffic through the streets of the city. Somebody, please kill me.

For the rest of the day, I hung out by the train tracks near my home. I thought seriously about jumping onto a passing freight train, but I didn't have the guts. Finally, about 6:30 P.M., I went home. Dinner was finished, and my mother had cleaned up the kitchen. And the way things worked in my home, if you missed the time when food was served, there were no second chances. My mother's only greeting was a mandate: Your father wants to talk to you.

Dad and I went out on the front steps of our tiny row house. I figured the high school had called, and my father confirmed it. He informed me that he would be accompanying me to the high school first thing in the morning for a meeting with the assistant principal about the trouble I encountered. Dad wasn't happy about any of this, primarily since he was taking the next morning off from work, which meant the loss of precious money for our family. Dad never inquired about the large bluish bruise on the right side of my face.

CHAPTER 1

He ordered me to bed, and I complied. But who could sleep anticipating the next morning at the high school?

I went into the closet of the bedroom shared by one of my younger brothers and me, closed the door, and sat in the confined darkness. I was listening to my tiny radio featuring Jerry Blavatt, Philadelphia's Rock n' Roll Geator. The music of the Four Tops and The Temptations coupled with Geator's Jive Talk were a great consolation to my overtaxed brain. When the Geator eventually went off the air after midnight, I cried myself to sleep in the closet. My life was in shambles.

The showdown session at the high school in the morning was nothing like what I anticipated. There was no sign of the idiot Brother Ricardo who had bashed me. Brother Dennis, the disciplinarian, and Brother Thomas, the assistant principal, wasted little time in apologizing profusely to my father and me for the previous day's misunderstanding. They spoke of their determination to rid the high school of the crud element that would vandalize a student's locker.

And then Brother Dennis informed my dad and me that I was immediately being transferred out of Brother Ricardo's class. At least I wouldn't have to confront any further irrationality from that moron nor face the roomful of student faces who had relished such a great show at my expense the previous day. I felt a little better, but not good. The high school was still ominous. The scars on my psyche from cold and unsympathetic students during this episode were permanent. My dad shrugged it off and went back to work. I was sent back to class.

In the four ensuing years of high school, I struggled mightily with survival, both as a student and as a human being. I weathered some nasty incidents with bullies as a freshman and sophomore, which Sal and Rocco, even though they had dropped out of school at the end of their sophomore year, finally helped me to remedy forever early in my junior year. This unfulfilled school discipline for those who had been terrorizing me was delivered emphatically by Sal and Rocco and yours truly back in our neighborhood using our own laws of the street.

Eventually, though, with my two old friends no longer being in school with me, I despaired. I became a high school loner, introverted, sullen, and uninvolved. I managed to stay in the college preparatory program, but I was predictably demoted from the elite honors class to a middle-of-the-pack honors class. I kept to myself, despised the cliques of various student groups, and avoided trouble by being street smart—staying two steps ahead of the bad guys. I never attended a prom or even a school dance, nor was I engaged in any school activities. I just came and went and finally finished. It was not a happy time.

To this day, my old high school celebrates its proud history. Many of its former students have succeeded in the public and private sectors. Numerous old grads return for reunions, communion breakfasts, and the annual beach blast. They share happy memories of times together in the great school they attended. I would never presume to question their positive experiences or their sincere fondness for the old school. However, all of this is completely foreign to me.

My high school life of isolation might well have crushed me. Who knows why it didn't? Or how close I might have come to emotional devastation. Could I have reacted to everything that happened to me with violence or some other unacceptable behavior? Quite possibly—but I did not! Instead, perhaps as a coping mechanism, I became my own island, a small piece of rock in a perpetually stormy sea. Not the healthiest of situations, but I survived. I decided that I would make my mark in life as an educator. And I also came to care very deeply that future students in any school would not have to experience what I did. The human fragility of any student is not to be underestimated. For how easy it is for a young person to become a nonentity. And how critically important it is for school staff members to intervene, to reach out with sensitivity and love to help a kid in trouble before he or she is lost forever.

2

JOEY GOES TO COLLEGE

Having completed high school in June of 1960, it appeared that I now had three career choices. One was to attend Philadelphia's La Salle College (now La Salle University), which had accepted me for admission as a member of its Class of 1964 beginning in September of 1960. My second option was to get some legitimate and immediate money working alongside my father in the huge General Electric switchgear plant located right in the middle of my Philly neighborhood. And then there was my top choice of a job: numbers running (conducting illegal neighborhood gambling) under the direction of Guido, the neighborhood bookie.

However, sometime in that summer after graduation from high school, Guido authoritatively reduced my options by insisting that I go to college. "For God's sake, Joey, you're one of the first guys around here who was even able to get admitted to a prestigious Catholic college like La Salle—why would you throw away that opportunity?" Guido explained. "Besides you'll be a representative from us people in the real world. You didn't have no silver spoons growin' up. You could be a role model for others. You could inspire more kids from this neighborhood to reach upward. And what a difference you could make as a teacher or a principal for kids who grew up like you did. So just forget about working for my business. It ain't gonna happen. At least not until you give this academic bullshit an honest shot!"

Nothing like a moral lecture from a rackets boss. Guido further issued a challenge that maybe I was just plain scared of trying to succeed in higher

CHAPTER 2

education. Of course he was right. But he also stirred up my competitive juices. Guido kept hammering me about equality, saying that people from our neighborhood deserved the opportunity to attend college like anyone else. "Joey, you can compete with anybody." Guido had this deal of my future education all greased and ready to roll. He stopped by my house on the steamy July night I filled out my acceptance confirmation agreement in front of my mom and dad and mailed the packet to La Salle College. The three adults were jubilant. I felt that I had just walked out onto a shaky limb.

When Labor Day arrived in early September, I hadn't heard anything from La Salle. I had been checking the mail religiously every day for weeks, assuming that my college classes would be starting soon and I was positive that I would be notified. I guess this wasn't too bright, but what did I know? Finally, my mother took matters into her own hands and called the college first thing on Tuesday, the day after Labor Day.

It wasn't good news. Orientation for La Salle's incoming freshmen class had been the previous week. Didn't we get the information in the mail? Classes would begin in two days. Send your son to the campus today and we'll try to sort this out.

One hour later, driven by panic, I raced out the door headed for La Salle College via trolley car and connecting subway, my only means of transportation, for a meeting with the dean of students. It was hot as hell. I was wearing my father's wrinkled black suit at the insistence of my mother. No time for ironing, just get to the La Salle campus pronto! The damn suit was also two sizes too big. And I was sweating like a pig. My drooping attire fit the image of the sad sack who had missed orientation. I was demoralized before I even started.

The preoccupied La Salle dean of students was distracted with new school year logistical problems in his beehive office of chaos. He spent two minutes with me apologizing for the snafu, and then handed me over to a senior class member who was supposed to provide me with peer enlightenment about the college. It was a bad plan. This preppy upperclassman had no time for a worthless frosh dressed like a nerd. We kept stopping at different spots around the campus where he chatted animatedly and at length with friends while I stood there ignored like the village idiot I was. I wasn't too impressed with my guide. He was an elitist, self-centered fool!

Predictably, after three hours, I had learned nothing. I still had no idea where the library was or how to access it, nor where the different classroom buildings were located, nor even how to find the bookstore or the cafeteria. Finally, this airhead senior dumped me back at the dean's office. Thanks for nothing! It was late afternoon and the place had quieted down. The dean had disappeared. Classes started tomorrow. I paid my first semester tuition, an awesome amount for someone from my social class ($300), picked up my fall roster of courses, and went home badly shaken.

My first days of college had mixed results. The good news was that I was able to navigate my way to each of the five scheduled classes on my roster. The professors seemed to be very nice. Classes were generally small in size and teaching involved "give and take." And I was struck by the manners of collegiate classmates. People said hello or nodded to you like you were a person. When you entered a building or a classroom, the student before you actually held the door until you got there instead of letting it slam in your face. This was a new world to me and I liked this part of it.

The bad news had to do with, of all things, textbooks. In my elementary school, books on different subjects were given to students free of any charge and then returned to the school authorities at year's end. High school followed much the same ritual with only a token book fee charged at the beginning of the school year. To my amazement, college was a different ball game. You had to buy your own books! Say what? How was I supposed to know this or deal with it?

I had carefully budgeted the precise amount of money for the first year of La Salle's tuition. Student loans would get me through the next three years. There was nothing left to buy books. And after attending my first five classes, I was numb at the fact that my professors had mandated eight different texts. Eventually, I searched out the La Salle bookstore and observed the long lines of students purchasing textbooks. I was doomed. I priced my required materials. The cost was somewhere around $100, an awesome amount for someone who worried about thirty cents of public transit money for the subway each day.

To this day, I believe that La Salle should award me some sort of honorary degree for my first-year academic achievement. I finished with a 2.5 academic index out of a possible 4.0. What's so remarkable about this accomplishment is that I did not purchase one new book during my first two semesters of college. True, I was able to acquire a couple of the mandated books from upperclassmen who no longer had any use for them and had

CHAPTER 2

them for sale at dirt prices. And I did buy another textbook at a bargain price from Leary's secondhand bookstore in downtown Philadelphia. But for the most part, I winged it.

Sometimes I got lucky and was able to temporarily acquire a precious text from either the La Salle or the Philadelphia Free Library. But usually, when classmate friends ate lunch in the cafeteria or sat around the campus in leisure, I borrowed (begged for) their books and read as rapid fire as I could. For the most part, I went through my freshman year at La Salle without the majority of the required books ever being in my possession. To this day, I get chills when I think about this. In my subsequent college years, part-time summer jobs and donations from Guido solved the book purchasing problem, but my first year at La Salle was an academic nightmare I would never wish on anyone.

In retrospect, maybe things would have been better for me at La Salle if I had just had the precious orientation information at the outset. But I doubt it. It wasn't anybody's fault but my own. College was another planet for me. I was an alien whose lack of money and social background handicaps were major detriments. Not that there weren't plenty of other working-class stiffs at La Salle during those times. I can only speak for myself. For me, it was all swimming upstream. Through it all, Guido was always there for me. On the congested streets of my neighborhood, he and I talked a hundred times during my four-year college adventure. Guido held me up, picked me up, and sometimes beat me up, depending on what I needed.

After more than a year of trudging through meaningless academic highways at La Salle, I finally found some refuge in a superbly taught English novel course. So many of the works we had to read (every one of them mercifully accessible from libraries) featured social class discrimination, hatred, revenge, betrayal, power struggles, violence, and deception, sort of like growing up in my neighborhood. I had found some relevance at last! I became a student for the first time in my life. And of all things, an English major!

To La Salle's credit, it was the only institution of higher learning that would dare to accept me into academia, something several other Philadelphia area colleges refused to do. Furthermore, the college nursed me along to finish a bachelor's degree in four years, a miracle the Vatican should perhaps investigate. For this, I will always be grateful. And then of course, there was the irrepressible Guido! In simplest terms, without my bookie advisor, college for me would never have even happened. Mentoring matters monumentally, especially for young people who need it the most. Empathy, support, motivation, and positive reinforcement from an adult who genuinely cares can change a life!

3

DISILLUSIONMENT OR DETERMINATION

When I entered La Salle College in 1960, there was an aura of optimism and idealism that pervaded the country. John F. Kennedy was a charismatic, inspirational president, challenging Americans to care about others less fortunate and to give of themselves to make a better world. It was a message that had great appeal to young people like myself and a far cry from today's version of the American Dream. Back then, the Peace Corps overseas and Volunteers In Service To America in our own country were booming with thousands of dedicated young volunteers. And I couldn't wait to become an underpaid teacher in the inner city where I could make some impact on kids in need.

But by the time I was graduated from La Salle in 1964, JFK had been assassinated. And that, of course, was only the beginning of the crash. Shortly thereafter two other prophets, Martin Luther King Jr. and Robert Kennedy, were blown away. The country was tearing itself apart with divided sentiments over the war in Vietnam. And Richard Nixon ascended to the throne of American political power in 1968. The late 1960s were not the best of times.

Indeed, most accounts of U.S. history during this period are focused on the hippie and flower power movement. Certainly, many young people turned to a drug and sex counterculture where authority (especially government) was despised. But that was not the only story of the times. Millions of other young Americans stayed the course of idealism.

CHAPTER 3

The beautiful Joan (who would become my wife in 1967) and I worked as teachers amid the urban challenges of the Camden (New Jersey) Public Schools at that time. We were undeterred. We were determined to make positive differences through quality education for the underclasses and also by advocating civil rights for people of color and cleaning up the polluted environment all across the United States. We were far from alone in this. Joan and I had lots of friends who shared our dreams. None of us took drugs or abandoned our priorities. And across the nation, numerous kindred spirits were doing the same things we were. It's a largely untold story in American history.

Joan was employed as a history teacher at Camden's Woodrow Wilson High School during those days. The student body was one-third Caucasian, one-third African American, and one-third Hispanic, an explosive mix of race and class in the late 1960s. As turbulence roared through America with riots and protests in the streets during those times, Woodrow Wilson High was just one more powder keg. I remember one period in particular during which I dropped Joan off at school each morning as National Guard troops stood on the front steps preserving order among students. Have a nice day, dear!

During one student walkout from classes, Joan's marvelous rapport with kids became apparent. She was the only one with whom the student walkout leaders would negotiate. With the school principal literally hidden behind locked office doors, a mini-skirted, long-blonde-haired, twenty-three-year-old Joan hammered out an agreement with hundreds of angry kids in the school auditorium and managed to get everyone back into class. This was no small feat. I always tell people that Joan is really Joan of Arc reincarnated, so I've never been surprised at her magnificent feats. Thinking big has always been her thing!

Joan was assigned the toughest, lowest-tracked students at Woodrow Wilson High because, amazingly, she could handle them. She was also given one honors elective course with complete freedom to establish the subject matter. She let the kids decide on the content for the course. After much debate, the class decided to pursue comparative religions. Each student would have to orally explain the tenets of one religion of their choosing in a class presentation and bring a representative of that religion to visit. It had to be a day to remember when two handsome male Mormons touched upon the inferiority of African Americans as well as the presiding Caucasian female teacher to their rainbow audience. These two young missionaries were quite lucky that they had Joan of Arc to escort them safely from the class.

By any measure, the comparative religion course was a great success. Joan and I scheduled a series of weekend field trips to attend sample services at everything from a synagogue to a Protestant fundamentalist church. And we probably learned as much as the kids. So who was voted best religion? Well, that really wouldn't be either ecumenical or a very sound exercise in a public school classroom. However, privately, with no mention to the students, Joan and I were greatly impressed with the Quakers . . . low on ritual and high on community outreach and concern for those less fortunate.

One of the most amazing places in inner-city Camden those days was a large home owned by two cohabitating teachers, Allison and George. They were an integrated couple, a generally despised oddity of the time, but Joan and I were enamored of them. That's because they were two of the most caring and decent people we ever knew.

Allison and George had an open door policy for Wilson's students. Joan and I spent many hours in their home marveling at what the two of them did for kids. We tried to help out where we could, but Allison and George were masters of their trade! During the evenings and all day on weekends, scores of young people would just show up. Bring us your tired and your weary of Camden—the emotionally upset, the physically abused, the substance abusers, those on the run, the hungry, and some just seeking out an adult who would listen. Allison and George always had time for everybody. They were a couple of saints, living the true definition of the word *holy* each and every day!

Joan and I did our share with Camden's street-savvy kids as well. We were counselors and parent figures to a host of needy students. When we discovered the real-world interest of some troubled youngster—art or music or sports—we often set up field trips to take the kids to some event across the river in Philadelphia that we knew they would enjoy while we played the roles of big brother and big sister, respectively.

In our most daring venture, we sponsored and chaperoned the first-ever trip to Europe by Camden high schoolers. Lots of friends and colleagues told us we were insane, which in retrospect we probably were. But we pulled it off splendidly, from raising the necessary funds, to getting the students

CHAPTER 3

safely back and forth to Italy, to making sure that the whole experience was educational and not frivolous.

Teaching in the Camden Public School System was formidable, demanding, and sometimes heartbreaking. It could be uplifting one day and devastating the next. Joan and I quickly discovered that beyond the daily routines of preparing lessons, delivering subject matter, and grading papers, there is so much more to being an effective educator. Quality teaching is certainly about opening the minds of students, but also their hearts and souls. It is often about helping pupils struggle and grow through the trials of life inside and outside school. Teaching is not just a job. It is a vocation, a calling to make a difference for young people. Great teachers live this every day.

4

THE POLITICAL FACTOR

The 1970s were a time of career chaos for me. Clear direction? Solid planning for the future? More like blowing with the wind! I left the Camden Public School System after six years because it was what I needed to do. I was exhausted; saving kids had drained me. I needed therapy. I found it as La Salle College's director of sports information. For five years, I was enveloped by a fantasy job of competitive games and cheering crowds. Great fun, but frivolous as hell. My conscience finally got the better of me.

I returned to the public education arena as the director of communications for the Upper Darby School District, an inner-ring suburb located just west of Philadelphia. It was my goal to become the great communicator for this community of just under 100,000 residents. Do a good job educating students, and then tell people about it—that's what it was supposed to be about. In my dreams!

Instead, my school board bosses wanted me to be the minister of propaganda. We'll do whatever we want any way we want and you'll make it work with mystical public relations skills. Oh sure, Joey the Magician! And so I spent five years trying to make the bad and the marginal and the questionable look good. I hated working with this corporate modus operandi. I also hated myself. I was badly compromised. I planned to exit this school district as soon as I could.

And then fate struck, big time. In 1980, conflict with the school board and a subsequent heart attack ended the career of Upper Darby's long-term superintendent of schools. Mike became the new boss. He planned to change

CHAPTER 4

many things. And he thought that I was a prime example of wasted potential and that I had been used the wrong way in the past. Mike promoted me, got more money for me than I could ever have imagined, listened to my ideas, and gave me power as an assistant superintendent for personnel and public information. Idealism and doing the right thing were once again put on the front burner. I was reborn.

By this time, I was also pursuing educational administration courses at the University of Pennsylvania's Graduate School of Education. Penn was a demanding place. I was forced to read prolifically in the field—divergent views of education, curriculum and instruction treatises by the ton, and gobs of material on management strategies and the political settings surrounding public schools. I assimilated, I analyzed, and I questioned. I became a serious student at the next level.

By October of 1984, I was a very content assistant superintendent. The Upper Darby School District was engaged in positive change on many fronts. Under Mike's leadership, quality education had replaced reducing school property taxes as the priority on the political agenda. A recently antagonistic school community had turned largely supportive. There was labor peace after a series of nasty clashes. I could have lived on happily ever after. And then lightening struck again. Mike was opting out of the superintendency after a mild stroke. This was very bad news. Even worse, Mike recommended to the school board that I become his replacement.

The superintendency was a job that I had never sought. And I wasn't sure I even wanted the position. The Upper Darby School District's immediate challenges for the future included a lack of adequate financial resources (due to a declining local tax base and shriveling state subsidies), growing enrollments with the accompanying need for new facilities, and substantial, ongoing demographic changes in the pupil population. None of this did wonders for my confidence.

On the other hand, I was being offered a magnificent opportunity to shape the educational future for thousands of students and ultimately the community in which they lived. How many educators would ever get this chance? Emotion ruled. I was almost ready to accept the job. But not until I understood the political factor.

The one mysterious thing about Mike as the superintendent of schools for the last four years had been his relationship with the local politicians. He

THE POLITICAL FACTOR

was in pretty deep. I knew better than anyone else that he had sought out and cultivated these connections, but I didn't know much about the reach of that political power into the school system.

I was certainly aware that the nine elected school board members were each carefully selected by these Republican political powers who had an overwhelming voting majority in the community. Indeed, no one was ever elected as a school director in Upper Darby without the stamp of approval from the political machine. That reality didn't much bother me. At least municipal elections would never result in the massive upheavals of school directors that had so disastrously impacted so many surrounding school districts. Nevertheless, I was quite apprehensive about political interference in the day-to-day management of the school system. So much so that I was ready to turn down the offer of the superintendency if I was going to be some kind of puppet attached to a tangle of political strings.

I was able to arrange a breakfast meeting with the powers-that-be in a local diner. I was scared to death and didn't sleep the night before. What in blazes did I know about dealing with a political power structure? The next morning, at 7:30 A.M., Big John, the legendary leader of Upper Darby's powerful political machine, his lieutenant, the senator, and yours truly sat in the diner's back table reserved for such purposes. Heavy things were about to come down. I ordered scrapple and eggs to gear up my Philly toughness.

I screwed up my courage and made myself very clear. "You guys are giving me an opportunity I could never have even dreamed of. I really am very honored and grateful. But I can't possibly function with a bunch of people micromanaging my every move. So if that's the way it's gonna be, it ain't gonna be me."

Big John was the obvious leader of this group. He nodded, smiled knowingly, and winked at the senator. Wave goodbye, Joey, I thought. This superintendency is going through the trap door.

But then, Big John's response astounded me. He looked me straight in the eyes. "If we had planned to micromanage every move of our superintendent of schools, then we would put an idiot in the job, and God knows there's plenty of them in the school system." Big John roared with laughter at his statement and was joined by his two colleagues. He then continued: "But this community is on the ropes with money problems. The student body is growing and changing. We need someone with brains to handle the

CHAPTER 4

challenges of the years ahead. That's why we want you in the job. Now before you think this is all nicey-nicey for you, let's get real here. What's in this for us is that good schools are good for our politics. When schools and all other services to the community are solid, we're solid . . . politically! You'll have your freedom because we both want the same things, maybe not for the same reasons but ultimately we're together in this."

End of serious discussion. I quit while I was ahead. Big John then proceeded to tell a series of very funny jokes, which I subsequently learned to be his trademark. Everyone laughed heartily! I gobbled down my scrapple and eggs with delight, and two nights later I became the Upper Darby School District's superintendent of schools.

During my fourteen-year tenure, I probably had a hundred contacts with the political powers. This is certainly not some unilateral recommendation for school leaders, but in my situation, there was no choice. Luckily for me, Big John turned out to be a bright, articulate, benevolent dictator. As promised, there was no micromanaging. And I actually liked meeting with him. Many educational administrators and school board members from across America will be horrified to think of such a practice by a school superintendent. But contrary to the conventional wisdom, my strategy of political interaction was smart, pragmatic, and beneficial to the school system. I needed to dance with the devil to get done what I needed to get done—and I got away with it!

Mostly I spent lots of effort keeping everyone on the same page regarding our schools, for it is a dangerous practice to have local politicians getting secondhand information regarding public education in their community. Sometimes I would apprise the political leadership of a potentially volatile situation. Sometimes I actually strategized and problem-solved together with politicos over some complex issue that threatened to blow the community to kingdom come. Sometimes I was asking for help or advice. This was not a pathway for amateurs. But in my situation, in my school community, it was what I had to do! And today, when I look back on all of this, I would not do anything differently. Communicating with the political power structure can be as vital to an educational system as communicating with parent constituencies, a clergy roundtable, a civic organization, or a vested interest school group.

5

WALLY WONDER

When I first heard that Wally was coming onto the Upper Darby Board of School Directors, I was filled with apprehension. His reputation had preceded him and it didn't sound good. He was a successful executive from big business, supposedly very outspoken, and an archconservative philosophically. I had also heard on the grapevine that Wally was a combat veteran of the Vietnam War and that he was nobody to mess with!

Surprisingly, Wally and I got on famously. He impressed me from the beginning with his strong support of quality programs for our students. That's because it turned out that he was one of our high school's graduates, and he really did care deeply about Upper Darby's young people and the community they came from, the one where he also lived. Wally turned out to be respectful, inquisitive, and studious about school district matters. Because of his financial background in business, he became a tremendous asset to the school district in money matters. On top of all that, he was very bright. And then I got a glimpse of his formidable side.

On a school board meeting night in the fall, the Aronimink School, located next door to our administration building where the school directors met, was simultaneously holding a "Back to School" night for parents. It was about 6:30 P.M., and Wally and I were the only ones in the administration building's board room, each boning up on the multiple reports that would require action when the 8:00 P.M. public meeting would commence.

We were soon joined by Harry, our school board president, a mischievous Irishman who had that twinkle in his eye that I knew spelled trouble. Harry

CHAPTER 5

rolled his eyes as he told Wally and me that one of the parents attending the "Back To School" night atAronimink School had dared to park in the reserved and clearly labeled parking space for the board president. Harry then laughed with glee as he explained that he had blocked that intruder's automobile with his own car so it couldn't be moved.

Harry had obtained that car's make and license number and then stopped off in the main office at Aronimink to request that a public address announcement be made over the school's intercom that the designated car be immediately moved since it was illegally parked in the board president's space. Harry delighted in the fact that when the perpetrator would go out to move his car in just a few minutes, it would be impossible since Harry's car now blocked the way. Wally and I just looked at each other with disbelief. Gee, there's not enough trouble in the world. Let's just go look for more!

Sure enough, within five minutes a giant, fuming, red-faced parent stormed into the board room and faced Wally and me who were sitting at the board table. The raging monster got right to the point: "I'm looking for the idiot who has my car blocked. I'm going to teach him some manners. So which one of you is the moron who did this?"

Harry, who was standing behind the angry parent, instantly saw the stupidity in what he had done and quickly fled out the door to immediately move his car. Meanwhile, I wondered if Wally and I were about to die. And then I saw the dark side of Wally. He stood up, and with a look of unblinking and glaring death the likes of which I have never seen, calmly addressed the invader: "You're making a big mistake with that kind of attitude," Wally quietly directed. "You really don't want to look for trouble you may not be able to handle. What you want do want to do is take a couple of deep breaths, walk out of here, and go move your car. Go back to the school and learn about your kid's education. That's why you came here tonight. You don't want to get involved with something you can't finish."

My heart was pounding. I was saying the Act of Contrition, preparing to meet God face to face at last. Wally just waited quietly and confidently, never breaking eye contact with the intruder. It was like the best Clint Eastwood movie you have ever seen. The problem was that I happened to be in the middle of this one. Thank heavens this parent had a meltdown. He decided to follow Wally's suggested course of wisdom. A sane decision! He turned abruptly and exited the board room. No doubt his car outside was no longer barricaded. By this time, I was hyperventilating. Then, like nothing had happened, Wally looked over and said to me: "These board reports for the public are in really good shape. I think that we're going to have a great meeting."

Over the years, Wally never ceased to amaze me with his classy demeanor and his staunch advocacy of Upper Darby's pupils in public. However, he was also a player behind the scenes. Several years after he had left the school board, Wally telephoned me and told me about a mentoring/scholarship program that he had heard was operating in the School District of Philadelphia. He asked if I could find out more about it, so within a few days I was at the office of Philadelphia Futures. It was a great program for which some of the most impoverished Philadelphia School District kids with academic potential were selected in ninth grade. A corporate sponsor promised a small scholarship to each designated student upon successful completion of high school, and even more important, provided an adult mentor through the four-year high school experience.

I reported to Wally that I absolutely loved this program. Then I dropped the bad news on him. Philadelphia Futures welcomed affiliates in this endeavor but also owned some sort of property rights on this initiative and required a $10,000 replication fee for anyone duplicating the program. Wally knew our school system's budgetary limitations as well as anyone; he also never hesitated: "Should I bring my personal check over this afternoon, or would tomorrow morning be okay?" Wally was going to make this happen!

The Upper Darby School District's Sponsor A Scholar program was born shortly thereafter. Since its inception in 1994, 108 (and counting) of the Upper Darby school community's neediest youngsters have benefited from the mentoring and scholarship assistance provided by a host of donors, ranging from businesses to individual teachers and administrators to civic associations. It is a spectacular program, unrivaled among greater Philadelphia's suburban school districts.

Wally's generosity went far beyond this. Every single Christmas, during all of the fourteen years I was Upper Darby's school superintendent, he and his wife issued a check of at least $1,000 to my Student Assistance Fund for needy kids. Wally never wanted any publicity for this. Meanwhile, his money touched the lives of scores of Upper Darby students, working miracles for those who couldn't afford some enrichment or remedial or other academic or personal enhancement program.

CHAPTER 5

Finally, I should note that Wally was the only one who I have ever seen who gave our local politicians what they truly deserved. As the state's share of funding for public education perpetually declined year after year through Democrat and then Republican administrations, and as Upper Darby's student enrollments grew year after year, local property taxes had to be substantially raised annually to make up for the shortfall of state financial support. Ironically, our local legislative delegation of state representatives was never too good at looking in the mirror at their pathetic role in this debacle.

One of the greatest joys of my life was watching Wally talk to these political culprits as only he could. At one backroom session of substantial seriousness, my school board leadership was using its traditional politeness as it danced around the issues of inadequate school funding from the state with our senator and two representatives. Same old boring, getting-nowhere stuff. And then, suddenly, Wally exploded. He gave our elected officials a tongue-lashing with enough expletives to make a sailor blush. It was vintage Wally. I loved every scathing minute of his diatribe. It hardly changed the state's abdication of responsibility for its fair share of school funding. But his words of condemnation to our legislative delegation were long overdue and on target! One of my fondest memories.

In subsequent years, long after he had left the school board, Wally became one of Pennsylvania's leading proponents of tax reform regarding public education. He relentlessly reiterated that the Commonwealth needed to establish new progressive taxes at the state level that would move local school communities away from the regressive property tax systems that were killing them. Today, many Harrisburg legislators have actually absorbed Wally's message, and some sort of public school funding reform is finally on the horizon.

In summary, you should never be too quick to judge anyone or anything especially on the basis of secondhand information or preconceived notions. In this case, I plead guilty. Wally ranks high on my list of dedicated and caring school board members. I would never have guessed that this could happen in a million years. Wally and I became good friends because we admired and respected one another. And who would have ever predicted that? It is the irony of ironies that I often thank heaven for all of the good that Wally brought to my school district.

6

GETTING THINGS DONE!

Sometime in the early 1980s, I attended a seminar on time management conducted by Ivan Fitzwater, a marvelous guru on that subject. His thinking influenced me profoundly as a superintendent. To this day, I am one of his staunch disciples.

After attending his seminar, I began my workday by getting up much earlier than I really had to in order to allow time for thinking in the quiet of my home before I went to work. For example, I usually would rise at 5:30 A.M. and then be showered, shaved, dressed, and sipping coffee on the porch or in some interior nook before 6:00 A.M. The next half hour was dedicated to a sort of meditative contemplation . . . no newspapers, no blaring television or radio, and no interruptions. This was my magical time. Each morning, I focused on my work, short- and long-term, as well as my philosophies of education. Like the finest Buddhist monk immersed in solitude, I often found solutions, saw visions of necessary change, and discovered clarity in puzzles. And even when that did not happen, I gained spiritual peace of mind. Almost always, I departed for work calm and unfrenzied, and I was in the office each day by 6:45 A.M.

Thank God, I have always been a morning person. Because in Ivan Fitzwater's philosophy, mornings are vital periods to school leaders. I ardently followed one of his simple rules. Get 75 percent of what you have to do each day done by noon. There is nothing random here. It's a bias for specific actions. Each morning, I would address a list of things to do that I had

CHAPTER 6

religiously left on my desk the previous afternoon before I departed work. Everything from meeting with individuals to telephone calls to writing necessary memoranda and letters. Usually by midday I had erased the list. Additionally, I had cleared the top of my desk.

For the most part, I tried to deal with any piece of incoming written material just once—to either forward it, file it, delegate it, assign it to myself, or trash it. I got it off the desk because, sure enough, by around noon, an equal or greater number of replacement pieces of new things to read and do would arrive. Finally, my afternoons were reserved for dealing with the unexpected, which usually occurred throughout each and every day. Keeping the afternoons open wasn't always possible, but at least by doggedly managing the targeted stuff every morning, there was some breathing time left to deal with people problems and educational issues each afternoon.

Public education is certainly a people business. But too often people contacts evolve into yet another time-wasting disaster. This is not to say that listening and nurturing and discussing are not critically important qualities for any school administrator—they are. But in far too many cases, phone conversation and office visits take up much more time than they really need to. And how much daily social conversation has contributed to a school leader being buried in paperwork or put behind schedule?

Minutes add up to hours. The clock needs to be controlled! I have never had much empathy for the administrator with a desktop covered with paper or one who is perpetually trying to meet deadlines. In most cases, that administrator is the guilty party, not the workload. Simply put, the management of time is often what makes or breaks a school administrator.

One of my initial edicts as a superintendent had to do with meetings of central administrators and principals. When I announced the imposition of a one-hour time limit for these meetings, colleagues were generally incredulous. This new superintendent was crazy! (Not the first time that had been suggested.) But this wasn't open to debate. Yes, meetings are important. However, I was prioritizing principals getting back into their schools where they belonged and central administrators getting back to their desks or out in the field as soon as possible. And so, after I gonged a few meetings to an abrupt close when sixty minutes had expired, no matter who was speaking or no matter what was being discussed, my mandate became reality. Eventually the culture changed. Meetings became much more crisp and focused.

And wonder of wonders: The school district actually survived in spite of a one-hour meeting rule.

One other area of time management concern has to do with the school board. The Upper Darby Board of School Directors was quite generous in convening on several evenings each month for sessions centered around general school district business and crisis management. However, it was almost impossible to engage in any significant consideration of long-term issues at these evening sessions.

For this reason, what was to become an annual board retreat took place for the first time in the late winter of 1983. A decision was made to go off-campus, out of the community, to focus on future planning for an entire weekend. Board members, central administrators, and select principals headed for the seclusion of a nowhere hotel outside of Lancaster, Pennsylvania, some forty miles from the school district. A tightly packed agenda was established for all day Saturday with a follow-up session continuing Sunday morning and ending at noon. All that was scheduled for Friday evening when participants arrived was a formal dinner and a social evening. A hospitality suite was set up in one of the hotel rooms, and board members and administrators furnished it with a wide array of spirits. In retrospect, a very bad idea!

After a hearty Pennsylvania Dutch dinner, highlighted by some brief remarks from the board president about the purposes of this unprecedented retreat, the attendees adjourned to the hospitality room. Initially, there was much camaraderie and good will. But the night dragged on and on. I went jogging. When I returned, the party was still in full swing, complete with uproarious laughter and glazed-over eyes. Going to bed was forbidden. We were all just one happy school district family. Finally, about 3:00 A.M., everyone retired to their rooms. I smelled a disaster. Our retreat sessions were set to get underway at 8:00 A.M., in just five hours.

Amazing what three or four hours of sleep won't do for you, especially after a night of imbibing. The group from the previous night of festivity was hardly recognizable—lots of red eyes, sour looks, and grim faces, is known in the vernacular as hangovers! By 9:00 A.M., the first arguments began. And through the morning of presentations, board members were nit-picking and jabbing and jousting administrators. We were plummeting downward, headed for disaster. I delivered my presentation of recommendations for

CHAPTER 6

more effective public relations in the future and got my head handed to me. I joined the ranks of the crucified. Finally, at 5:00 P.M., the board went ballistic and ordered all of the administrators except the superintendent (Mike) out of the room. We waited outside like sheep listening to much yelling and screaming inside the meeting room from which we had been evicted. The verdict soon arrived.

We were informed that the school board was generally displeased with the quality of all of the administrative presentations. Sunday's agenda was canceled. We would reconvene back in the school district every night next week until we got it right. So much for all-night cocktail parties! This was a lost weekend!

Well, with enough sleep and time having passed, the iceberg thawed. What we were supposed to have accomplished in a cordial weekend retreat we had to hammer out in three successive weekday nights of tension and hard knocks. All of us had learned a commonsense lesson: that booze and intelligent planning never mix. And little did I ever imagine that in the ensuing months, Mike's health would be compromised, he would depart the superintendency, and I would be the superintendent of record for the next retreat.

Twelve months later, Mike was gone. The now dreaded annual school board retreat was about to occur. There was great fear and apprehension among my administrative staff. This called for drastic measures. I invoked the Joey Doctrine for Survival. Administrators shall not drink at this event! The hospitality room was abandoned forever. The hotel bar was off limits. We were on duty! A program was developed with a guest speaker for our opening dinner on Friday night.

Apparently our school board was equally determined to put the debacle of the previous year's retreat behind them. They resembled a convention of Alcoholics Anonymous, true models of sobriety. Ironically, that disastrous retreat of the previous year was a watershed for the Upper Darby School District. Much good arose from the bad. We were able to set clear educational directions for the future. Administrators fielded a flood of board questions. There was time for in-depth discussion of issues. There was give and take. We established a sense of common purpose. We were a board and its administration planning together as they should. Annual retreats became a very worthwhile staple for us!

7

CONSTRUCTION NIGHTMARES AVOIDED

It must be nice to take the time to thoroughly plan out a construction project for a school. It must also be nice to be able to borrow whatever monies are necessary for a first-class facility. I wouldn't know about either of those fantasies! My school district had a declining tax base, and we were always strapped for money. And then, when I assumed the reigns of the superintendency, new students began showing up out of the woodwork. So I spent my fourteen years at the helm trying to stay just a step or two ahead of the enrollment boom via one construction project after another.

All of this was further complicated by a lunatic taxpayer fringe group perpetually harassing the school board about avoiding new taxes. I had to be very certain that projected enrollments would materialize into real kids. Otherwise, the taxpayer zanies would nail me to the nearest cross. In addition to that, in a school district struggling financially, even if my school board could be convinced that construction was necessary, you can be sure that money would only be appropriated for the economy model.

My first construction project—the expansion and renovation of two elementary schools, each more than fifty years old, on the east side of our school district that bordered the city of Philadelphia—was memorable for two reasons. First, I gained the school board's approval for these projects by taking them on a school bus ride to each facility on a Saturday morning. Nothing can replace being on site. Six of the nine board members had never been inside these schools. When the school board saw the smallish size classrooms

CHAPTER 7

and dismal lighting (which would never meet state approval by present standards), the undersized library, gymnasium, and cafeteria, and the ancient student lavatories that carried a perpetual odor of urine no matter how well they were cleaned and disinfected, the project was unofficially approved that morning.

The other unforgettable aspect of these initial projects is that they were completed over one summer in a mad dash to destiny. Completely rehabilitated with additional classrooms, a new library and multipurpose room (gymnasium/cafeteria), new student lavatories, and a new office area, each of these schools could now house hundreds more students in modern, properly sized, and hygienic facilities. More than one contractor told us that these projects couldn't be done in such a condensed timeline over one summer. Oh, ye of little faith! Prophets of doom! Trademark of the construction business!

And so a modus operandi was created in the Upper Darby School District. Since there were no extra school facilities in which to temporarily house pupils, any construction was going to be initiated and completed over the summer vacation period. That was in granite! There was no other choice. During the school year, we fought the public battles with taxpayers for construction approval. We had the architectural plans drawn and approved by the state, completed the bidding process, hired the contractors, and finally brought the heavy equipment on site in the spring while the students were still in school.

But that was the easy part. I now established a team of key players inside the school district to engage in terroristic wars on contractors during the summer months. We gave our contractors many doses of screaming and shouting and legal threats that they were hardly used to from gentle school people. We won lots of Academy Awards. And we got it done! So what if I had a host of parent, teacher, administrator, and maintenance worker volunteers emptying hundreds of boxes of stored educational materials, sorting and creating order at the eleventh hour over the Labor Day weekend and even on Labor Day itself? Both schools under construction opened on time in September.

During my superintendency, the other building projects included two complicated and intense expansions of the senior high, the resurrection of one formerly closed elementary school, and the physical transformation of another previously closed elementary school into what has now become the model kindergarten center in the greater Philadelphia area. The scenario was always the same. I used the same independent consultants to justify the need for construction via enrollment projections. We could certainly have generated this information in the school district by ourselves, but the outsiders brought objectivity and a sense of validity to the public approval process. This set in motion the series of preliminary logistical requirements, and then all hell would break loose during summer construction.

For every project, I had the benefit of the same school district team in place. These key players became quite adept at the intimidation and coercion skills necessary to get something built in a timely fashion. Walter, a senior citizen school board member who was a World War II combat veteran and an expediter by profession before he retired, badgered the architect, construction manager, and individual contractors relentlessly and unmercifully on the work sites; he loved every minute of it. Michael, my supervisor of maintenance, was as street smart as anyone you could find about materials and workmanship; he was a tough, mad-dog micromanager of every component of the construction. John, another school board member who was a retired engineer by profession, became my expert watchdog on blueprints and schematics being carried out to specifications. Ken and Ed were my school district's business manager and purchasing agent, respectively; their mission was to make sure that every construction dollar we spent was justified, or in more simple terms, to make sure no contractor ripped us off. Barry, the district solicitor, perpetually dangled the threat of lawsuits before any misbehaving contractors. As for me, I just meaningfully meddled and stirred the construction pot as necessary. I did my best to appear unstable. My top achievement was when I threw a fake tantrum, used every curse word known to man, and smashed a lamp against a wall near the general contractor's head when he was being uncooperative.

Not to say all of this was absent some fun. After one of the miracle construction projects was completed at the senior high, my team and I were emotionally drained, as usual. I wanted to reward my school district key players with a feast in a wise-guy restaurant in the heart of South Philadelphia's Italian section. Sal and Rocco made the arrangements. They wanted me to take the key players to the restaurant in one of their limousines, but I declined. Beware the appearance of evil!

CHAPTER 7

The word was put out in South Philly that this was a private party, so we were the only customers. Mama Fran and her son cooked everything to order that night, a spectacularly delicious Sicilian feast accompanied by enough homemade red wine to fill a lake. I'm sure that my key players had to wonder about the lack of other patrons in the restaurant. But this was to be our private celebration. It was all arranged. To complete the evening, a wonderful vocalist sang every Frank Sinatra song ever made while we gorged ourselves. It was a grand evening. Cost me a few hundred. Worth every dollar!

In conclusion, construction projects in a school district are usually among the most difficult and volatile obstacles for a school board, a superintendent, and staff. So based on my vast experience, I humbly present you with the gift below:

JOEY'S TEN GUIDELINES FOR AVOIDING CONSTRUCTION NIGHTMARES

1. Never believe any architect or contractor regarding timelines for construction.
2. Assume the worst in any construction project. Prepare everyone in the project under construction well in advance for chaos and disaster.
3. Neither a construction manager nor an architect nor a clerk of the works is adequate to deliver a project on time. Put your own team of gorillas in place for this purpose.
4. Have regular public presentations about construction timelines at school board meetings to keep contractors on the frying pan.
5. Never be nice to contractors; they consider such behavior to be weakness.
6. When necessary, act like a lunatic!
7. Have your solicitor consistently threaten legal action against contractors.
8. If required, conduct a press conference about contractor incompetence.
9. Pray to St. Jude For the Hopeless.
10. Hire Sal and Rocco to get any construction project back on target!

8

ETHICAL CONSIDERATIONS

I once wandered into the office of a colleague and found him holding and admiring a beautiful picture frame made of high-quality stained wood. "Nice frame," I brilliantly stated. I was always the master of clever small talk. "Was it expensive? Where did you get it?" I had run out of stupid things to say.

"Oh no, it didn't cost anything. Our maintenance shop made it for me," he replied with empty-headed delight. "I just gave them the custom specs and they let me pick from their array of wood choices. And, believe it or not, here it is only two days later. Just look at this workmanship."

So maybe I tend to overreact sometimes. I avoided throwing this subordinate out of the nearest window, although I was sorely tempted. I downshifted into a slow burn. "Now let me get this straight," I quietly began. "Have you been in the same meetings with me where our principals keep telling us that their work orders are months behind schedule? How does our shop have time for picture frame building? But let me ask you something even more important. You have just taken advantage of taxpayer-funded labor and materials for your own personal purposes. Have you lost your [deleted expletive] mind?"

The scorched administrator looked at me with glazed-over eyes like I was some idiot. I watched his amoral mind spinning its secret thoughts. Didn't I know how the world worked? Blue-collar guys doing anything to get in good with white-collar guys. You scratch my back and I'll scratch yours. It's just a fringe benefit/job entitlement.

CHAPTER 8

To help him get the point, I offered some emphatic direction. "By this afternoon, you will have requested and been given and paid in full an itemized bill from our maintenance shop for labor and materials for your gorgeous picture frame. You will also advise those misguided workers who did this for you that in the opinion of this superintendent of schools, they should be prioritizing the zillion work orders that affect schools and children and teachers. Be sure and tell them that I haven't asked for their names and that's lucky for them! Because if this ever happens again, I'll be looking to terminate people." I stormed out of the administrator's office and slammed the door for effect. I wondered how many more half-wits were in my army of followers.

Such episodes involving ethical decision making have always intrigued me. The simple incident of the picture frame could easily have taken down this school administrator with a public scandal and a news media field day. There's enough jeopardy in the school leadership business. Why seek out more of it with stupid deeds?

One other infamous ethics tale from my school district occurred long before I was a superintendent. It involved, of all things, a certain annual, heavily attended weekend event at the senior high. Most people paid at the door, and when the event eventually concluded, there were several thousand dollars on hand. The event coordinators, two teachers and one administrator, then divided the total proceeds, and each carried a one-third share home. Sometime on Monday, each conspirator deposited his one-third share into his checking account.

On the next day, the threesome each delivered a personal check written to the senior high for the exact amount of his one-third share. No money was ever stolen, just laundered. And sure enough, several months later, each of the event coordinators deducted a documented charitable contribution to the senior high on their federal tax returns. The net was a few easy bucks. A simple victimless crime. No harm done. Everything clean as a whistle. At least until the Internal Revenue Service and the school district caught the three perps.

All of this was incomprehensible to me. I knew each of the three people involved and liked them all. As far as I knew, they were decent, caring educators. What were they thinking? How about arriving at a simple conclusion that this is wrong and I'm not getting involved? How could this easy money be worth the kind of risks they took? Demotions, disgrace, and heavy fines soon followed. A pile of human rubble!

ETHICAL CONSIDERATIONS

Over the years, as a superintendent of schools, I have noted with interest much more serious accounts of fraud and ethics violations in school districts nationally. Often, I would convey such news stories to my principals and administrative staff. But those violations always seemed distant, unreal, and far from our daily realities. And then things hit closer to home.

In 1999, the scandal lid blew off the pristine teapot of an affluent neighboring school district. A school board investigation had led to an independent audit, which had uncovered more than $160,000 of alleged unauthorized spending by the office of the superintendent for Japanese artifacts and related services. Say what? What in the name of the bizarre and the misappropriated was going on in that school district? Someone who sat three chairs away from me in monthly meetings of our county superintendents was doing *what*? The local press had many banner days with this one. And needless to say, my reaction to this farce led to all-time spikes in my blood pressure. I became a raging volcano.

There are few institutions that have the open scrutiny and visibility that exists in a publicly financed school system. It is common for taxpayer watchdog groups to harass and demean and challenge the school district administration at monthly school board meetings regarding spending and financial management issues. In Upper Darby, where educational dollars were scarce and needs were many, we had our share of taxpayer wackos constantly seeking mud to sling and even inventing it when it wasn't there.

For that reason, I carried a whip and wore black leather boots for my fiscal oversight duties in the school district. My business manager, Ken, who had been sent to me from heaven via the private sector, was my kindred ally in cajoling, demanding, and enforcing strict financial accountability from each and every administrator. We were very proud of our clean management, and we had never lost a battle over any fiscal oversight issue with the taxpayer complainants.

And then there was this idiocy in the neighboring district. First of all, from an equity vantage point, it made me sick. As my school system struggled to obtain and wisely appropriate every precious dollar in the best interests of our students, this fat-cat rich district nearby was in flames because its superintendent had been regularly purchasing very expensive Japanese artifacts and services with taxpayer monies. It was ludicrous and despicable.

CHAPTER 8

I called a meeting of my administrative staff and principals. I ranted and raved about Japanese swords and scandals that colored all educational administrators as crooks. I used a colorful array of curse words. It somehow seemed appropriate for this occasion. And I have never seen so many open-mouthed, shocked administrators. But I think my position was very clear on this matter.

As for the superintendent perp in the nearby district, he soon resigned in public disgrace. His lawyer promised that full restitution would be made. I could care less. The damage had been done to the credibility of every public school district's fiscal management operations. About a month later, I was visiting a professor friend in the educational leadership department of the University of Pennsylvania. We chatted about the demise of this superintendent colleague whom we both knew. My friend told me that he had great empathy for the ousted superintendent and wondered what we could do to support him in his time of need. I bit off a piece of my tongue, choked on it, and withheld all the invective I could. This ethics stuff certainly needs a lot more work with practicing school administrators and the professors who teach them.

Perhaps the most heartbreaking case of an ethical mistake and a subsequent disaster also occurred close to home. In another school district, just a few miles from Upper Darby, a female school administrator had achieved a difficult plateau for women: she became the superintendent of schools in this college-town community. Promoted from the inside, Jan had done this the old-fashioned Smith Barney way: She had earned it! I knew Jan from monthly meetings of the University of Pennsylvania Study Council for Superintendents. I found her to be bright, engaging, well-read, and thoughtful. I was disappointed and surprised when she departed her Pennsylvania school system after only two years for a superindendency in Weston, Connecticut.

That was all I knew, especially since I took early retirement in June of 1999. And then, about two years later, I read about her tragic demise in the newspaper. In late April of 2001, Jan's cleaning lady arrived one morning and discovered a note on the front door telling her not to enter the house but to call the police. Inside, the law enforcement officers found that Jan had hanged herself.

ETHICAL CONSIDERATIONS

This is an ugly story. Jan was a dedicated educator, only forty-eight years old at her death. Immersed in trying to do her best in her new post with the Weston schools, a piece of her past had followed her. It became public that in her former superintendency in Pennsylvania, Jan had been the subject of an ethics investigation for accepting more than $15,000 in gifts from a contractor employed by the school district. With this disclosure, she became a lightening rod in the Weston community. Some of her supporters argued that Jan had acknowledged the mistake and paid a fine and that the matter should be closed. But her detractors used this incident to ignite their closet searching for more wrongdoing and to demand her removal from the superintendency. It was Weston's very own witch trial. Shortly thereafter, Jan ended her life.

Certainly, the incivility of this small Connecticut town obsessed with being judge and jury is an example of human savagery at its worst. In contrast, there is a much more humane lesson from the Pennsylvania school community where Jan had previously served as superintendent; her memorial service was packed with mourners who celebrated her accomplishments as an educator, the good that she had done for so many in her life. But sadly, there is also the ultimate truth that any compromise of integrity by a school leader is never worth the potential consequences. And an ethics violation is seldom repairable.

9

JUST A FEW THOUGHTS ON TEACHERS AND TEACHING

I admit to having very strong feelings about what constitutes good teaching. Most of my bias, as you might expect, comes from my personal experience. I have been heavily colored by the good, the bad, and the ugly. And like the sensitive sponge that I am, I have absorbed it all and processed it into an educational philosophy.

There were teachers who gave me encouragement and self-confidence. There were those who showed me fairness and patience. And there were some great motivators. But, alas, there were also those who were incompetent at class management. There were those who were terrible communicators of their subject matter. There were far too many who specialized in criticism and had no concept whatsoever about teaching all the children. And finally there were those who specialized in fear and degradation of students.

Some twenty-two years ago, when I first began graduate studies at the University of Pennsylvania, I ran smack into the ideological treatises of an avowed Marxist professor. This professor universally condemned schooling in "capitalist America," noting that public educators in general are validators of the socioeconomic inequalities that pupils bring with them to classrooms.

I adamantly disagreed with this professor at that time. Shortly thereafter, however, I began very reluctantly to see some validity in his arguments . . . certainly not in his generalized condemnation of American schooling, but in one underlying premise about quality teaching in his overall argument. This professor argued that there has been and continues to be too much rubber stamping of kids in schools. And I happen to agree with that premise.

CHAPTER 9

Mediocre teachers all too often end up validating a youngster for what he or she is at that time, never looking at what this kid might become. Students who show up with academic talents and initiative tend to do very well. Average pupils stay lost in the middle. And pupils who arrive with "baggage" are in trouble from the outset. These mediocre educators label these young people predictably. To support their alleged objectivity, they eventually support their assumptions with quantified results (tests). This process destroys too many kids with needs and blasphemes against the nature of teaching itself.

In contract, great teachers are change agents. They find the positive "turn on" switches in those kids who to others seem lost. Where this student is at present is not what matters. Where can I take this young person becomes the driving force. Great teachers use encouragement and praise and positive reinforcement to turn lives around, to get all students, regardless of ability level or personal problems, to reach for heights, to go where they might not have ever been before, in quest of some educational success story.

Sometime in the early 1990s, I attended a seminar sponsored by the American Association of School Administrators (AASA). An inspirational speaker was scheduled for one of the morning sessions. I planned to skip it. I needed "nitty-gritty" as a superintendent of schools, not some cheerleader. But my Catholic guilt got the best of me.

I grudgingly dragged myself to the meeting room. There on the stage was an odd-looking fellow, dressed in some sort of colorful outfit. I knew I shouldn't have attended this session. I despaired. Somebody, get me out of here! But how very wrong I was. For this speaker, Dan, turned out to be powerfully poignant. After sharing some humorous anecdotes, he went "autobiographical" and told us of the polio that had stuck him down at seventeen years of age in the prime of life as an athlete and student leader among peers.

Dan contracted polio the year the Salk vaccine hit the market. He lost the use of his legs and one arm and most of his body. But he finished high school and proceeded on to college to follow his dream. He couldn't run . . . he couldn't jump . . . he couldn't do so many physical things that all of us take for granted. Yet as a college freshman, Dan courageously told the head of the physical education department at his university that he wanted to be a physical education teacher.

I shared this story of Dan many times over the years via memo and speech to Upper Darby's teachers and administrators. My punchline to district educators was always the same: What would have been your response to Dan? What would any of us have said to this supposedly pathetic young man about his college goal? For heaven's sake, we have to be realistic here. Let him down softly, but do it! Would we have squashed his dream? Would we have validated his "inadequacy"?

So here's the punchline. Some thirty years after Dan initially professed his dream to become a physical education teacher, his physical problems weren't any better. However, in his home, Dan now displayed the numerous awards of excellence he had received for his superb career as a physical education teacher. He had retired as a distinguished school principal. In his leisure, he had learned to fly his own plane, play guitar, and master golf. All of this accomplishment had occurred because some key people viewed him for what he might become—not as a flawed human being—and had refused to validate his supposed limitations.

During my years in the Upper Darby School District, the challenges to our teaching staff were formidable. Certainly, there were thousands of students who came to our classrooms with strong academic skills and firm backing from the home. However, we also had large numbers of pupils who had transferred into the school district from nearby Philadelphia seeking the promised land; many of these young people started out several grade levels below their new peers in reading and math skills.

Additionally, Upper Darby's schools became the refuge for large numbers of immigrants who had flocked from their native lands with their children to a community with affordable housing and good schools; there was an abundance of language and sometimes cultural problems to overcome with this group. In yet another area of challenge, the school system educated by far the largest population of special education youngsters among the fifteen school districts in Delaware County. And finally, with so many parochial and private schools operating adjacent to Upper Darby's public schools, there were always numerous transfer students. It is true that some of these pupils were academic standouts, but many had either fallen far behind academically or been problem children who were asked to leave these parochial and private schools.

As a school leader, nothing had a higher priority for me than trying to encourage and inspire our teaching faculties to care about and make a best effort with every student. Perhaps my most famous address to the school

CHAPTER 9

system's approximately one thousand staff members focused on just that point. I delivered a speech using four boxes as my subject matter. One was a beautifully wrapped masterpiece of a gift box, set off by many glittering bows and ribbons. Another plain white box was decorated with just some ribbon and one bow. The third box was enclosed by brownish postal wrap and tied with twine. And the fourth box was enveloped by newspaper which had been crushed and torn to shreds. I emphatically told the audience of teachers and teacher assistants and secretaries and school principals that each of these boxes (students) had dreams and hopes. But how many of us would treat each of these boxes without discrimination, believe and work with each of them equally?

That message sunk in quickly. And it stayed. On hundreds of different occasions in later years, teachers would stop me in different schools and talk about the lesson of the boxes! And I would like to think that this lesson became a guidepost to our school system's collective and individual thinking about the young people we served.

Paul Houston, the executive director of the American Association of School Administrators, has defined the epitome of educational effectiveness as "helping our children dream and live as fully and completely as they can. More than anything else, education is about giving wings to children's dreams" (*The School Administrator*, May 2002). In the ideal, students might come to classrooms with strong parenting, well-loved and cared for, and with middle class values and some basic academic skills. But our world is far removed from that ideal. The mission of the truly heroic educator is to push the youngster who is achieving well to even greater heights, to build achievement in a student who has been written off by others, to light some fire for the average, to give hope to that pupil who has no hope, to love the kid who has no love, and to always be a dream builder, not a dream breaker.

10

SPECIAL PROJECTS

After getting lots of best wishes, plenty of advice, and promises of their willingness to help me from Sal, Rocco, and Guido when I became Upper Darby's superintendent of schools in the fall of 1984, I hadn't heard anything from my three old compadres for many months. Undoubtedly, they were busy with the press of illegal business! Then in June of 1985, the four of us had dinner together at Ralph's, a hundred-year-old family fixture restaurant in South Philadelphia.

We had an Italian feast and drank lots of red wine. It felt good to be with my old comrades and away from school district problems. And then Sal dropped a bomb on me. He had an agenda: "Joey, next September, you're going to get a new student who's really important to me. She's a relative whose life has been filled with nothing but trouble. Angelina is the daughter of a cousin of mine. This cousin and his wife are convicted drug pushers who are addicted themselves. As a matter of fact, they're also headed for the pen. Angelina has just been assigned by family court to another of my cousins, Richie, a decent guy with three little kids and a nice wife, who lives in, of all places, Upper Darby.

"Angelina needs to be saved, Joey. She's had three strikes against her from birth. She's a goddamned mess, but what else could you expect from living in that house with two parents who are bums? Angelina's only fourteen years old, Joey. She'll be a ninth grader with your schools in September. She'll be in the best home she's ever had. She needs a new start. All I'm askin' is that you take your best shot with her."

CHAPTER 10

I assured Sal that I would do everything I could for Angelina. I certainly owed Sal big time for a few favors he had done for me over the years. But I was also intrigued by this kid in trouble. Trouble was something I knew about firsthand. I resolved to save her.

In late August, when the thousands of academic rosters were generated for Upper Darby High's students, I pulled Angelina's schedule to check on the teachers that she would have. Even though I was a relatively new superintendent of schools, I had been in the Upper Darby School District for almost ten years. I had firm opinions about just exactly who were the quality teachers at our senior high, the ones who related to all the students who came to them, not just the self-fulfilling prophecies. I wanted to make sure that Angelina would get a few of the best. I doctored her roster, arranging for Angelina to have Manny and Laurie, two dedicated teachers of academic subjects who truly loved their students and literally bled the school colors of purple and gold.

Shortly thereafter, I invited Manny and Laurie to my office for a private meeting where I informed them that they were two of the best teachers I knew. I next told them about Angelina and that I had selected them to be her guardian angels for her first year at Upper Darby High. The two teachers first looked at me with disbelief, but not for the reason you might think. Laurie explained that she and Manny had never known any administrators at the top level who had any idea of the real-world problems of kids at the high school. She was very moved to see a superintendent who was a human being. Of course they would work to save Angelina. Manny and Laurie and I bonded together that morning with a unified purpose.

For the first month of school, I had been receiving regular progress reports of Angelina from my two teacher disciples. The word was that she was going to be a tough nut to crack. I had casually visited one of her classes without giving her any indication that I knew all about her history. Her spiked punk hair, black lipstick, and multiple earrings made Angelina stand out even among high school peers. Even I was spooked!

Then disaster nearly struck. Sometime during a late October weekend, Angelina disappeared from her new home. She had departed on a Saturday afternoon and had not come back twenty-four hours later. Her guardian, Richie, and his wife were frantic. They notified the police. They also contacted Sal, who pulled me into the loop. I then telephoned Manny and Laurie who gave

SPECIAL PROJECTS

me their best educated guess that Angelina had gone to her favorite hangout, South Street, Philadelphia's Mecca for far-out teenage types.

Within an hour, Sal and Rocco and I were meandering down that famous street where all the hipsters meet, seeking out our lost soul. It looked like a gala Halloween party all around us and we were out of costume. Sal and Rocco were wearing black leather jackets to cover the hardware strapped to their black turtlenecks underneath. I had on my Boston Red Sox hat and my brown leather jacket and dark sunglasses, doing my best imitation of Robert Parker's Spenser. We questioned a hundred teenage aliens before we hit paydirt. Finally, one of the South Street wild things informed us that he knew Angelina and that she was almost certainly with her friends in a second-floor apartment up the street. How nice. Sal and Rocco and I would stop in for tea. This group was about to have some unexpected Sunday visitors.

When we arrived at this den of iniquity, the door was open. Too bad—it would have been fun to break it down. Inside were all sorts of spaced-out teenagers strewn about the one-room apartment. Ah, the marvels of booze and drugs. Angelina was passed out on a sofa. One oversized macho druggie clown pulled out his knife, jumped up, and ordered us to get out. Rocco smoothly decked him with one right-hand punch. Rocco then confiscated the teenage thug's knife and waved it menacingly, informing the assembled group in very colorful language that Angelina was leaving them forever by decision of a higher authority. Anyone challenging this decision now or later would have to cope with the wrath of Rocco! The glazed-eyed group appeared to get the message. By this time, Sal had Angelina up on her feet and leaning heavily against him. We exited quietly with what we had come for.

Nobody back in Upper Darby ever thought Angelina was going to be easy. We all just resolved to do better. There were no quick fixes! Tough kids just don't get hit by lightening bolts of values and academic prioritizing. It's all about patience and caring human support mechanisms. It's all about incremental change, one day at a time. It's about resilience in the face of setbacks. Over the next four years, I engaged many other members of my professional staff on the Angelina project. It was all uphill. Gradually, she became a part of Upper Darby High School. By graduation, four years later, Angelina had miraculously progressed to the point where she had not one suspension during her senior year. And she was headed for the Delaware County Community College to study computer science.

CHAPTER 10

With all of this exhaustive effort to significantly change just one pupil, it became crystal clear to me that more extensive and sophisticated intervention efforts were a school district requirement. In the late 1980s through a state grant, the first student assistance teams were set up at the Upper Darby High School. Later these intervention units were expanded to also function in our two middle schools. Since that time, these groups of volunteer professionals have been targeting students with all sorts of problems from substance abuse to emotional and other adjustment problems. It has been a remarkably effective program, a source of great pride in the Upper Darby School District, and a tribute to the many dedicated educators who have prioritized saving kids.

11

A DOSE OF NEW THINKING, PLEASE!

Through much of my superintendency, a series of high-powered conferences and blue-ribbon commissions on educational improvement seemed to be ongoing at the national level. What's so amazing to me is that, for so many of these meetings, the attendees were corporation executives and state governors.

Someone has to be kidding here. I just love the corporate executive model of excellence that prioritizes greed and materialistic gain at all costs. Perhaps we should develop a new education manifesto using the wisdom of those recently indicted and convicted CEOs. How admirable and moral so much of it is!

1. Profit rules over any other considerations inside or outside the company. Just lay off thousands of loyal workers when poor management decisions have caused financial problems for the corporation. Or cut back on the quality of materials or workmanship, resulting in defective or unsafe products, when economies are necessary.
2. Use every deceptive type of advertising known to man to con the corporation's publics, from the consumers to the shareholders to the news media.
3. Ignore government regulation as much as possible in the name of cost savings, especially those expensive mandates that affect the quality of the workplace inside the company and the quality of the environment outside those insulated corporate walls.

CHAPTER 11

4. Cover-ups are a wonderful first line of defense, but if necessary, subvert the legal process. And, when all else fails ...
5. Cook the books.

Ah yes, the business model! What a wonderful track record to incorporate into America's public schools.

Then, of course, we have those paragons of immoral wheeling and dealing, our political and governmental leaders. From Abscam to Watergate to Iran-Contra, what stellar examples for our young people to emulate. Influence peddling, mismanagement of public funds, twisting and turning of truth by staff propagandists, bribery, cover-ups, and outright lies to the electorate. And these are the same people that tell us that schools are broken!

Most of these leadership figures have spent little if any substantial time in public school classrooms, observing teachers and students and learning dynamics. Likewise, most have had little or no contact with principals and other school administrators to discuss the realities inside our schools. And because the vast majority of these leaders and executives live their lives amid the upper-class trappings of mansions and yachts and exclusive golf courses and protected ivory-tower work environments, how could they possibly understand the demographic and socioeconomic challenges inherent in those thousands of public schools far removed from their affluent public school counterparts and private schools?

So what kind of nonsense is going on here? Where are the teachers and principals and superintendents at these national summits? It's like convening a national conference on the state of medical practice in the United States and excluding the input of doctors and hospital executives or developing a wartime strategy by excluding the military from the discussions. This deliberate lockout of professional educators from the public education reform process is a disservice to the nation. Further, it insults and demeans those who work in the trenches of our public schools every day and have firsthand knowledge of the problems as well as ideas regarding potential solutions.

Listed below are some perspectives that for the most part have been ignored by our never-ending bandwagons of self-anointed and politically appointed experts on public education in America.

1. Forcing students to learn and coercing teachers to teach better via high-stakes tests is an absurdity. It is the product of the simplistic thinking of corporate executives and political charlatans. It conveniently ignores the fact that educational outcomes for our students are impacted by many other factors in our culture and society, not just schooling.

An analysis of the more than three million children that began school across the United States just a few years ago revealed that more than 20 percent were from poverty-level families, more than 10 percent were children of teenage mothers, more than 10 percent were physically or mentally handicapped, 15 percent were children of immigrants whose primary language was not English, more than 25 percent were children already living with a single parent, and more than 10 percent lived in a home where neither parent had finished high school.

What could be more naive than to argue that we will just test these students to greatness while ignoring the need for reforms both inside and outside of the schools? Before his untimely death, U.S. Senator Paul Wellstone (D-Minnesota), out of the mainstream of stupid thinking prevalent in the White House, Congress, and gubernatorial mansions, courageously decried the use of high-stakes testing as the panacea for educational improvement with these succinct words: "I find it amazing that testing, which was supposed to be a way of assessing reform, is now being treated as the actual reform."

2. Professor Bruce J. Biddle, writing in *Phi Delta Kappan* (September 1997), pointed to the extensive research about what creates such drastic differences in achievement among schools and school districts. *Inequitable school funding and poverty among America's children are two major culprits.* Our rates of child poverty in the United States are dramatically higher than those of other industrialized nations with whom our educational outcomes are often compared.

Tragically, too many government and political leaders like to keep their heads buried in the sand regarding these matters. These great pretenders ignore the realities and bash the public schools. It's certainly much easier that trying to address these nasty little secrets about socioeconomic disparities in the United States.

How ironic that business CEOs, for whom money matters more than anything else to drive the success of their enterprises, would dare to argue that for public schools, money is never the answer. It is the height of hypocrisy.

CHAPTER 11

And how ridiculous it is for state governors and legislatures, many of whom have betrayed their school districts with inadequate funding over many years, to now decry public schools and demand better achievement. The abdication of funding responsibility by the Commonwealth of Pennsylvania while I was the Upper Darby School District's superintendent of schools bordered on criminal. As the percentage share of state funding of public education radically declined through the 1990s, government "spin doctors" distracted the press and the public with tough accountability talk and high-stakes testing programs. In Philadelphia, when the lack of adequate state funding eventually brought that school system to its knees financially, the state took over the school system and then blamed the school district for everything from financial to educational incompetence. This was a classic page from the defense of a rapist: blame the victim. Pennsylvania government at its worst.

3. Researcher Gerald Bracey is one of America's most authoritative sources on what really matters in public schools. He has recently synthesized research in *Phi Delta Kappan* (September 2002) on the academic loss that poor students experience over the summer while middle-class and affluent peers either gain or hold their own. The implication is that no matter how well a school has done with poorer students during the academic year, *a summer spent away from school in a nonaffluent community with far fewer resources than its wealthier counterparts will have a significant detrimental effect educationally on these pupils.*

It is research like this that should be inspiring educational initiatives by the federal and state governments. If we really cared as a nation, we could easily stop this summer loss. And there is so much more that we know about what matters—from the need for universal preschool programs to before- and after-school educational day-care programs, especially for our most impoverished students.

4. Finally, the most profound study of forces outside the schools that affect educational results comes from a massive research study of Laurence Steinberg and two other colleagues, Bradford Brown and Sanford Dornbush (*Beyond The Schools*, 1996). Among their findings are the following:

- For a large segment of American students, just "getting by" in school is good enough. This group devotes little energy to academic pursuits, and many students almost never read outside the school environment.

A DOSE OF NEW THINKING, PLEASE!

- Nearly one in three parents in America is seriously disengaged from his or her adolescent's life, and especially from that adolescent's education. Approximately one-third of students say their parents have no idea how they are doing in school.
- The glorification of stupidity in the mass media has downgraded the importance of academic and intellectual achievement in our nation.

A key point of this research is that "for far too long our national debate about the declining achievement of our students has been dominated by disputes over how schools ought to be changed without simultaneously examining the other forces in students' lives that affect their willingness to learn and their ability to achieve."

In summary, American education has plenty of problems these days. Ongoing reforms inside the schools are essential. However, *high-stakes testing has never been and is not now a reform*. Many of public education's problems are outside the schools. As long as inadequate school funding and poverty prevail, as long as our government makes only minimal efforts to bridge the gaps between haves and have-nots educationally, the priority needs of American schooling will not be significantly addressed. Indeed, we have lost our way when testing has become the panacea for our nation's schools.

America must take a hard look at itself and stop unilaterally obsessing about schools. We must find ways to encourage and rekindle and if necessary demand greater parental involvement in schooling than currently exists. We must review what our society prizes on television and in the mass media, for these are powerful teachers of our young people. We need to find new heroes to emulate other than those often questionable figures in sports and entertainment. And finally we must have much better leadership and role modeling from the corporate and governmental arenas.

WHAT COMMUNICATION?!

In an address to the General Session of the National Council of Teachers of English Spring Conference in 1998, Towson State University professor Bess Altwerger examined the forces behind media and legislative attacks on public education and reading instruction. Her remarks are a call to arms for anyone who cares about public education across America:

> Almost all of the newspapers in this country are owned by six corporate giants.... Almost all of the media are owned by only nine corporations.... The media is no longer the voice of the American people but of American business. What are the educational goals of corporate giants, and how can these goals be accomplished by destroying confidence in public education . . . ?
>
> They want public funds to subsidize and expand private schools, which provide the legal means to achieve segregation of the poor and disenfranchised children of the public schools. They want a workforce from public schools that they can count on with a high level of basic skills . . . literate and competent enough to do the job, but not creative or critical enough to question the overall business agenda.... They want control over the goals and outcomes of public education, which is easier to achieve if the public believes schools are on the brink of collapse. And they want increased profits through the privatization and commercialization of public school instruction.

An outrageous thesis by Professor Altwerger? A fantasy? An unjustified attack against the free press? Not if you have worked in public education for a lengthy period as I have and have had to deal with perverse editorials, shallow

CHAPTER 12

opinion commentaries, and censorship of ideas and arguments that would dare to counter infallible newspaper positions on public schools. To me, Professor Altwerger's proposition rings very true!

Indeed, the recent state takeover of the Philadelphia School District has had all the elements of corporate manipulation. It began with the political execution of a superintendent of schools who was totally frustrated with the lack of adequate financial support for Philadelphia's public schools from Harrisburg. Then there was a railroad job by successive Republican governors and their legislative allies—the big push for privatization. City politicians were sucked into the plot with backroom deals and a quick fix of some one-time extra state funding. There was never any doubt that a private sector company, Edison, was going to be given Philadelphia schools to run, just a question of how many. In South Philly, some would call this a bag job.

Sure enough, when schools opened in September of 2002, the *Philadelphia Inquirer* (September 5, 2002) reported that the state and city governmental leaders roamed around Philadelphia together, "swapping praise, joking, laughing, and shaking pom-poms to commemorate their historic partnership."

I reacted angrily with a letter to the paper (September 6, 2002), which the newspaper declined to publish. Not surprising. I guess I should have grabbed my pom-poms and joined the celebration. Instead, in my correspondence, I termed this staged show of unity a hypocritical farce. Such a bad temper I have! Here's the rest of what I wrote:

> Were these politicians commemorating Pennsylvania's abdication of its funding responsibility to Philadelphia's schoolchildren over so many years, which has put the city schools in the dire condition that they are in today?
>
> Tragically, all of this public relations hoopla was hardly about quality education of Philadelphia's school children. Rather it is the dream fulfilled for an obsessive political power play focused on privatizing public schools nationally. Harrisburg has become a pathetic torch bearer, a driver of this corporate agenda, shoving the concept down Philadelphia's throat.
>
> And so a substantial portion of Philadelphia's public schools has now become the grand experiment for Edison, a company struggling desperately for its own financial survival with no significant track record of any educational success on the scale of what is being undertaken in Philadelphia. With a third-quarter loss reported at $49.3 million, and an accumulated deficit of $199.4 million since 1996, Edison is a shaky messiah at best. And they are only getting this opportu-

WHAT COMMUNICATION?!

nity to run schools in the city of Philadelphia because they have such good friends in the state political circles, city government, and the news media.

Too bad no one in Philadelphia got to read my dissenting commentary. But I'm getting used to it. The *Philadelphia Inquirer* doesn't seem to have much space for what I have written for several years now.

Anyone else might develop some kind of complex over this treatment. In my case, it just provokes me even more. So for the record, here's just a bit of my editorializing on this issue that was deemed unworthy to be printed:

> Throughout the Casey and Ridge administrations, Pennsylvania's school districts have been left to the political whims of Harrisburg politicians. The results have been disastrous. Pennsylvania once funded 50 percent of the cost of basic education statewide. It was widely viewed as the state's constitutional responsibility. Now that percentage of state support has declined to 36 percent, a betrayal of the Commonwealth's schools and the children they serve. As a result, the local share of support for public schools has had to increase significantly to the tune of one billion dollars of new property taxes as documented by the Pennsylvania School Boards Association.

It gets even worse. I was trying to mind my own business as a guest of the Rotary Club of Philadelphia for lunch in late July of 2001. That day's speaker was the Republican candidate for governor in Pennsylvania. He spent much of his time bashing Philadelphia's public schools, Harrisburg's favorite pastime. Another political genius! It wasn't a very intellectual presentation. Actually, it was dumber than dumb. I was also struck by the fact that a guiding Rotary principle states: Is It the Truth?

I wrote another letter to the *Inquirer*, that bastion of journalistic excellence that serves my city. My solitary confinement continued. Thou shalt not be published! So maybe my commentary might not have sat too well with some unseen Republican power players. But when did newspapers stop caring about the truth? From my growing scrapbook of unpublished missiles, I present you with this excerpted gem:

> On two different occasions, this speaker indicated that the Philadelphia School District was spending $10,000 for each student's education. This data

CHAPTER 12

was utilized as an illustration of the rather expensive output for public schools in Philadelphia and as a rationale for why the Commonwealth of Pennsylvania should not give any additional money to the Philadelphia School District.

Astonishingly, there is no factual basis to this guest speaker's cost figures. The Philadelphia School District's actual instructional expense per student is presently under $5,000. This can easily be verified from the research base of the Pennsylvania School Boards Association.

The Philadelphia School District is hardly a big spender. Its per-pupil expenditures rank significantly below the vast majority of suburban school districts surrounding the city. And statewide, Philadelphia's per-student expense ranks 270th lowest among 501 school districts.

In summary, this was an unjustified and unsubstantiated attack on a school system that educates some of the neediest pupils in the Commonwealth. The city's schools deserve fairer treatment and at least some minimal effort at objectivity from someone aspiring to the state's highest office.

Well, the good news is that this Republican candidate for Pennsylvania governor was soundly defeated in the election of November 5, 2002. But you also have to wonder if I may have become some sort of news media outcast. I don't really mind. I just don't get it. I thought thinking was allowed in America and that newspapers were a conduit for a variety of views and ideas. Well, let's push the conspiratorial thesis aside and just look at news media quality. George R. Kaplan, the author of *The Mass Media's Version of America's Schools*, offers this wonderful summary of the state of news media coverage of the 1990s:

> In a fantasy for the times, Moses comes down from Mount Sinai with the Ten Commandments, to be met by TV's most famous reporters. They interview him, and their stories are edited. Only two commandments make it to the evening news—the ones on adultery and coveting one's neighbor's wife.

There is no question that, during my years as a superintendent of schools, anything negative about the schools would always predominate over the positive. I once kept a documented record of potentially newsworthy items publicly discussed or presented at the monthly school board meetings over a one-year period. It was amazing that complainers, bitchers, and moaners, attackers and muckrakers, always got top play in the newspapers. School district achievements, initiatives, and innovations often got no coverage or were buried deep inside newspapers.

WHAT COMMUNICATION?!

And then there were those snide cheapshots fired broadside into someone's heart. One of the worst examples of an unjustified attack came from the *Inquirer* on the Upper Darby School Board's legendary president, Teresa. A dedicated public servant, Teresa would never miss a public meeting unless it was the most dire emergency. In the spring of 1996, she was admitted to Delaware County Memorial Hospital with a serious illness. For this reason, she was not in attendance at a public budget hearing, and some vitriolic citizen subsequently complained to an *Inquirer* columnist on the suburban beat.

The next day this exemplary model of journalistic prowess wrote in his column: "The board president didn't even care enough to show up to hear the testimony of taxpayers at the school system budget hearings." Oh sure, ignore the medical advice of your doctor, put your life at risk, and just have some hospital nurses drag you out of your sick bed and take an ambulance over to a school board budget hearing. If this slothful columnist had taken a minute or two to telephone the school district offices, he could have easily discovered the situation with this seriously ill board member. But this guy was too cynical or too incompetent, and after all, it's much more fun to use a newspaper column to crucify people. Justice . . . fairness . . . what does that have to do with anything? To make matters worse, when we notified this columnist of his blunder, he never put a retraction of his slanderous commentary in the paper. I thought seriously about asking Rocco to visit him, but then I concluded that this bum wasn't worth it.

Another of the great newspaper adventures of the mid-1990s occurred when the school district implemented block (intensive) scheduling at the senior high. As a result, high school students were now engaged in academic classes for 90-minute periods instead of the traditional 45-minute periods.

This restructuring of the school day had resulted from long-term study by a group of teachers and administrators who were meeting in afternoons to examine various ways to improve the high school. Eventually, after going on site to see the block schedule in operation in high schools where it was already in place, this study group, led by the school principal, recommended that our high school shift to the block schedule. A strong academic and school climate rationale for the change was presented in several public sessions with high school parents and later at several school board meetings in full view of the press. Nothing was rushed. And eventually, the block schedule was put into operation at the senior high.

CHAPTER 12

But no one could have foreseen that in some strange circles, block scheduling was equated with voodoo. It was condemned as an evil plot by some right-wingers and other fanatical opponents from Jupiter and Mars. And when the same three or four regulars from my community of 85,000 began beating the issue to death at monthly school board meetings, you would have thought that there was some major groundswell uprising. The news media covering the Upper Darby School District had a field day with front-page stories of the same few people singing the same strange songs month after month.

One of the opinion columnists at the *Inquirer* next launched a series of articles condemning the block schedule innovation. When it was our school district's turn to be put in the meat grinder, this columnist authored an article questioning the use of block scheduling at Upper Darby High School. Apparently, he obtained much of his perspective by attending one meeting of a handful of anti–block scheduling residents from several school districts. That was the basis of his article. He obtained their negative comments and views on block scheduling and wrote his column.

Just one simple question here. Controversy is certainly news. But shouldn't this journalist have made some effort to contact some representative of the Upper Darby School District for balance? For what his newspaper ended up with was a one-sided column that was shallow and biased. Of course, maybe that was what it wanted.

I should note that the same kind of prejudicial writing can occur when columnists do make contact to get the school district's side of some controversial matter. One of the other columnists for a local newspaper on the Upper Darby beat seemingly always developed his column with his deep-seated bias solidly in place. No counterarguments to his predisposed notions ever made a difference with this writer. Not surprisingly, he became a block scheduling basher as well.

I do have one brief and ironic footnote to this block scheduling news media debacle. In November of 1997, I had the opportunity to visit Sinclair High School, located in a suburb of Toronto, Ontario. That senior high was rated as the best high school in the world in 1996, defeating finalist schools from The Netherlands, Hungary, Norway, Scotland, Switzerland, and New Zealand. It was a pleasure to see the school in action, view their many innovative programs, and chat with teachers, administrators, and students.

WHAT COMMUNICATION?!

The Carl Bertelsmann Foundation, which conducted the competition, noted that Sinclair High School had a collaborative culture, integrated curriculum, powerful ongoing staff development, strong partnerships, and an active school community council. Oh, and one final note: This school used block scheduling as the basis of its educational delivery of services to students. After the ridiculous bashing we in Upper Darby had taken from the local press over this matter of block scheduling, there we were on common ground with the best high school in the world. It was with reluctance and some degree of insecurity that I authored a blistering indictment of shoddy journalism in our school district's community newsletter, circulated to 36,000 homes served by our school system in June of 1997. And then in my first book, *Yo! Joey!* (1999), I lashed out in several chapters regarding the quality of educational news coverage. As a result, my relationships with editorial rooms and reporters alike have never seemed to be quite the same. Now let me get this straight. School administrators are supposed to be perpetual pin cushions for the press. But school leaders are not permitted to criticize the news media. Isn't that called a double standard?

The best summary of the state of news media coverage of education was authored by David Berliner and Bruce Biddle in *The School Administrator* in September 1998. After intensively studying newspaper articles from around the country, these researchers concluded that the news media:

- Is biased and covers the negative side of news stories much more diligently than the positive side.
- Presents too simplistic and incomplete a view of the educational problems and issues that they are reporting.
- Is more critical of the schools in editorial policies than it is complimentary.
- Has editorial policies that are biased against public schools, school change, and, in particular, schools that serve the poor.
- Displays a lack of understanding of the complexity of school life in contemporary America.
- Shows an appalling lack of understanding of statistics and social science research, without which reporters cannot properly interpret the huge amount of data that the educational system produces.
- Shows an ignorance of the role of poverty as a root cause of many of the difficulties in our schools.

CHAPTER 12

The floodgates have been open for some time now. And the deluge of misinformation, distortions, hyperbole, and outright lies keeps flowing about public education. The news media has largely failed to be an effective communicator about schooling in America. And because of this horrendous inadequacy of the press, government bureaucracies with political motivations, vested interest groups of all stripes, a host of empty-headed talking heads on the electronic media, biased think tanks and other ivory towers, and right-wingers have an unchallenged free rein to color the thinking of the American people regarding public education in any way they choose.

All of this has very serious implications for public school leaders. I have termed it the *communication imperative*. Given the sorry state of news media coverage of public education, coupled with the emergence of so many self-anointed, highly questionable experts on schooling in America, new and enhanced communication by people who know public schools best—teachers, school board members, support staff, and school administrators—has become a critical necessity. For far too many of the wrong people these days have been telling Americans what to believe and think about public education!

The venue for this communication imperative is at the grassroots level. The messages can be effectively conveyed through that mass of personal interactions all of us have on a daily basis—in honest, straightforward, plain talk with parents of school-age children and with family and neighbors and friends, in stores and shops, in civic organizations such as Rotary and Lions and Kiwanis clubs, at cocktail and dinner parties, and at sports and entertainment events.

The public education advocacy agenda here is not all that complicated: to attain some balance against one-sided news media coverage, to counter outright lies and misinformation, to refute the simplistic, to help parents and citizens at large to focus on what really matters, to build and enhance understanding of public education's efforts with 90 percent of America's school-age population, and to make the case for improved financial support from state and federal governments.

13

HARRISBURG FOREVER!

I once heard a renowned demographer describe the citizenry of the Commonwealth of Pennsylvania as the least migratory among all of our United States. More than any other state, Pennsylvanians tend to remain in the state of their birth for all of their lives. The average age of Pennsylvanians is much older that most other states, and citizens are generally conservative. And that is why this demographer concluded this: Creative thinking is forbidden in the Commonwealth of Pennsylvania. He further explained Pennsylvania geographically as Philadelphia and Pittsburgh with a grand wilderness in between. Within that context, Harrisburg makes for a perfect state capitol. The place was a kind of jungle.

Harrisburg's politicians do all of their real business in the back rooms. That's where the deals are cut and decisions are made. Pennsylvania has a strict Sunshine Law thanks to its legislature, an alleged champion of openness of government when they enacted this law. Funny thing, though—the legislature exempted itself from having to hold its deliberations in full view of the public and the press like every other governmental body in the state. It was the height of arrogance and so typical of Harrisburg politics.

I must admit that I have never liked Harrisburg. How could I? This was the home of governors and legislative bodies that I grew to despise. During my superintendency, the funding streams for public education lost their flow. I can't even politicize this thing because the decline of statewide support for basic education began under Democrat Governor Robert Casey and continued under Republican Governor Thomas Ridge.

CHAPTER 13

But in heavily Republican Delaware County where my school district was located, all of us had high hopes for some improvement in school funding when Ridge was elected. I remember a classic meeting in our county that brought together school board members and superintendents with the elected state representatives from our area. It was one year after Ridge was swept onto his imperial throne and school funding had still not improved.

The legislators on the podium hemmed and hawed, noting that it didn't look good for any increased funding from the state for our schools. There wasn't too much they could do! Their comments should have incited a riot. But we were a congregation of devout Republicans. Even though all of us were desperate for more state money, politeness prevailed.

And then everything changed forever. A school board member from Lansdowne, the community next to Upper Darby, rose up to address the two politicians, the Republican leaders of the Senate and the House of Representatives in Pennsylvania. He was eloquent:

"I don't understand what is happening here. We elected Ridge to help us. You people who sit in the legislature are there to help us. Your Republican party controls Harrisburg and you don't know whether or not you'll be able to get us more money. What the hell are you people talking about? We're the ones who put you in office. Have you forgotten who we are?

"I have voted for local property tax increases for six consecutive years in my school district. And now I have friends and neighbors who no longer speak to me. Our school board meetings each month are filled with bitterness and hatred, which was never there before. And that, gentlemen, is your fault. For you have betrayed us, our schools, and our communities. You are colossal failures."

The two legislative princes sat before the audience of more than two hundred constituents in stony silence. Both had red faces. I loved every minute of it. And I marveled at the courage of this speaker who had tearfully expressed so well what all of us were thinking but were afraid to express. The two politicians whispered to each other, and then, without a word, exited the room. This meeting was over. As a matter of fact, all future meetings of this kind were also over. This annual elected official-school board breakfast, a longstanding tradition, would never occur again. The poor little politicians were offended!

One of my other fondest memories of beloved Harrisburg is the voucher battles. Thomas Ridge came into office determined to steamroll a voucher program that would provide stipends to students attending private and parochial schools through the Pennsylvania legislature. This initiative was a priority goal of the national Republican party and would launch Ridge into the limelight for presidential consideration in the future if he could pull it off. Intense pressure was exerted on legislators from the governor's office. Propaganda machines were operating full force.

One of the dumbest tenets of the voucher proponents was that for each public school student who used the voucher stipend to transfer to a private school, the public school from which this pupil departed would save the per-pupil instructional cost of thousands of dollars. The simple-simon thinking of Republican strategists. For each student no longer in your school system, the district saves a ton of money. Basic Enron accounting methodology!

I got into some heavy newspaper wars with Ridge's local legislator point man, Billy, who kept publicly arguing that he couldn't understand my opposition, given the fact that vouchers would save my district tons of money. I tried to explain things to Billy to no avail. At that time, Upper Darby's per-pupil instructional expense was about $5,000. In Billy's theory, if one of my second graders transferred to St. Whatever School, my district immediately saved $5,000. So check this out. If 28 students are in one of my second grades and one departs, where exactly are these big savings? I still need the classroom, the teacher, the heat, and the lighting. For Billy's math to work, hundreds of students would have to leave for private schools. Then we could at least be able to eliminate some teachers, which are the heftiest part of the cost of instruction.

However, on a more realistic plain, the fallacy of this Republican mythology was that, with six national schools of excellence among my twelve and a richness of curriculum opportunities built into our senior high programs, Upper Darby's public schools had been attracting numerous students away from private and parochial schools. None of them were about to transfer back where they came from for a $300 or $400 bribe.

When the voucher vote was about to occur in Harrisburg, the backroom political heat was intensified for any Republican legislator who might out of conscience dare to disagree with this Ridge mandate. The Senate would rubber stamp the voucher plan. The problem was in the House of Representatives. There were a handful of holdouts who were all told the same thing: Your career as a legislator will be over forever if you don't vote with us on

CHAPTER 13

this. Think of the consequences. Is there anything that you need for your constituents that we can get for you in return for your vote? I know all of this because one of the targeted Republican legislators was a close friend and confidant.

In Harrisburg's finest style, this particular vote on vouchers occurred well after midnight. As the legislature's electronic voting scoreboard in the House of Representatives began to render its verdict, it suddenly became clear that Ridge was going to lose. This would be a terrible mark of failure on this gubernatorial emperor's presidential aspirations. Was not there some brave Republican knight in armor who could save the day? There was! One brave Ridge disciple literally pulled the plug. Tsk! Tsk! An electronic scoreboard malfunction! This vote was never official. And Ridge would live to lose on his voucher obsession again, which he did.

Not surprisingly, my respect for Pennsylvania government has been significantly diminished. Certainly the state capital has many well-intentioned and principled elected officials. It's just that the Harrisburg collective so often malfunctions and has certainly not been able to get its act together regarding public education for the past decade or so. More specifically, I will never forgive the state for its abdication of the responsibility to adequately fund Pennsylvania's public schools during the 1990s.

Today, when I watch the sessions of the legislature on Pennsylvania's cable network, I continue to be appalled. Speakers at the podium argue passionately for some cause over a din of noise that fills the chamber since a hundred conversations are happening around the room. Elected officials can be viewed reading newspapers or dozing off or conducting group meetings on some other subject matter. There are always lots of empty chairs. All of this because the real action is decided upon in secret chambers, not within the beautiful scenery of the legislative chambers and far from the Sunshine Law that regulates all other governmental bodies of the Commonwealth.

14

JUST A FEW WORDS ABOUT UPPER DARBY STUDENTS

During my superintendency, the Upper Darby School District had the largest K–12 pupil population among Delaware County's fifteen school districts. The overall enrollment grew from 7,600 students when I started my tenure to more than 11,000 by the time I retired. Our schools were large, not by choice but because of a lack of open space to build new facilities and a declining local tax base that required limited and prudent spending.

The culmination of schooling for all of our kids occurred at Upper Darby High School (grades 9–12), where all of our neighborhood schools eventually sent their pupils. The senior high student body that grew to more than 3,000 youngsters when I was superintendent was a tremendous mix of humanity in terms of social classes, learning abilities, family backgrounds, aspirations, and racial, religious, and ethnic diversity. The high school was always an awesome place to me. I never ceased to marvel at how well it functioned.

Our high school was organized into a house system whereby an assistant principal, a secretary, three guidance counselors, and some part-time teachers operated out of their own center and attempted to personalize the environment at each grade level. The house staff stayed with its class of students from the freshman through the senior years and then started all over again with an incoming group of ninth graders.

I must admit that I was always apprehensive about the senior high. But my fears were unfounded. This place was magical, a tribute to the dedicated

CHAPTER 14

teachers, administrators, and support staff who made miracles happen each and every day.

Commencement exercises stick out in my mind first and foremost. A typical graduation ceremony of 700 Upper Darby High students was conducted outdoors in the football stadium to accommodate as many as 7,000 well-wishers who might attend. To me, this was a ticking time bomb. Not because of anything in our schools, but because our society has become so uncivilized.

During the late 1980s and into the 1990s, there were many tales of graduation event disasters in surrounding school districts. Graduates acting like fools, carrying one another in piggyback fashion, cheering and guffawing and yelling like they were at some pep rally, not paying attention to commencement speakers, holding up stupid signs, and tossing hats, beach balls, and water balloons in the middle of the ceremonies. Added to this, the parents and siblings in attendance at these animal-house functions often exhibited worse behavior than the students. Perhaps unfairly, I blamed the colleges and universities for this kind of behavior, since I believe much of the high school graduation chaos of the times was modeled on what had previously been witnessed at higher education graduations for other family members. And too many of my administrative colleagues in nearby school systems just threw up their hands and tolerated this behavior.

Whatever the case, none of us connected with Upper Darby High were about to let this happen. The organizational aspects of these events were fine-tuned year after year with notes and suggestions handed down from class to class. The administration encouraged faculty members to emphasize dignity as a priority for graduation ceremonies in discussions with students.

Each year, the leaders of the senior center reiterated what was acceptable behavior to the graduates that they had come to know so well. It was an intellectual appeal directly to the seniors involved—coercion was never the primary means. For many, these would be the last graduation exercises that they would ever attend. And even for those going on to higher education, the commencement event was posited as a time to reflect on the past and look to the future, to mold a lasting, positive memory.

Oh sure, we had many robed teacher marshals creating a presence of law and order at each year's graduation. But even with by far the largest graduating classes of any high school in greater Philadelphia, I can never remember any significantly ugly incident, yet alone any mass chaos like that at other high schools. In summary, the stunningly beautiful and memorable Upper Darby High School graduations year after year were a tribute to the maturity and self-discipline of the seniors themselves. It was all about the values and behavior that ultimately reflected certain ideals. And that reflects so admirably on the influence of the faculty and school leaders at the school. Because I had never attended any proms or dances when I was in high school, I looked forward to dressing up in a tuxedo and taking my wife, Joan, to Upper Darby's senior proms when I became superintendent of schools. But I didn't know what to expect. For our first senior prom together, Joan and I arrived fashionably late and the party was in full swing at a large downtown hotel. Almost immediately, I was accosted by an armed security guard. "Ain't you the superintendent of schools? I got somethin' to say to you," he began. I braced for the worst. "Your kids are really somethin' else. Last week, we had a private high school here for a prom and they vandalized the hell outta this place. We spent that whole night takin' booze and pot away from those spoiled rich brats.

"But your young people are the exact opposite. This is probably the largest group of high schoolers I've ever seen here in this hotel. They've been respectful and polite and mannerly so that I've had nothing to do all night except watch them dance. Are you sure that you guys are from Upper Darby? Your community's supposed to be full of tough kids. We really expected to have our hands full tonight, but this has been just amazing."

I thanked the security guard for his comments and just wished I had a tape recorder with me. School superintendents and principals live to hear stuff like this. It filled my heart with elation. And I related it to parents and teachers many times over the ensuing years. Joan and I attended fifteen consecutive proms at many different locations. All of them were without unsavory incidents or problems and often the hotel managers wrote complimentary letters about our students to the high school administration and pleaded for them to return the following year.

I would be remiss if I didn't mention one final aspect connected to these proms. Upper Darby High School parents, concerned over post-prom activities involving alcohol or precarious driving trips to the nearby New Jersey seashore or heaven only knows where else, were among the first to establish post-prom parties back on the high school campus many years ago. Through

CHAPTER 14

their remarkable hard work, the majority of Upper Darby High's prom attendees now traditionally return to the high school when the hotel prom ends at 1:00 A.M. Our parents have found through trial and error and resilience the right series of games, food, dancing, and teenage fun to keep most of our seniors safe and sound through the wee hours of the morning right in our own backyard.

Finally, there are two other appraisals of Upper Darby High students I'd like to share. The first involved a visit of about thirty parents of students from a neighboring high school in an affluent community in the late 1990s. They wanted to see our block scheduling up close and personal as a prelude to its possible implementation in their high school. The high school supplied them with student guides and gave them free rein to visit classes of their choice. At the end of the day, the visiting parents were also able to debrief a cross section of ordinary students about their experiences with block scheduling. That was what I knew.

After their day in the school, the leader of the parent delegation telephoned my office and demanded to speak to me. This didn't sound good, but I reluctantly took the call.

"We just can't believe your students; they were such a delight," this parent leader said. "Our group insisted that I call you as soon as we returned home. We have never met such down-to-earth, sincere, and responsive young people. They're so human, and frankly we're not used to that. They interacted with our parents so well. Please convey this message to the high school faculty. You must be so proud."

I was indeed very proud! And you can be sure that I conveyed this message not only to the high school faculty but to the school board, all of our other principals, the central administration, parents groups, the Rotary Club, the clergy roundtable, and just about everyone else I ran across in Upper Darby.

My last snapshot of Upper Darby High students is from the sports arena. Not in powerhouse teams and rampant athletic success, although we have had some, but in sportsmanship. In evaluations of the conduct and demeanor of student athletes in all sports in our league competition by referees and officials, Upper Darby High was awarded the sportsmanship banner in four of the last five years before I retired. Nothing could have been more meaningful for our many sports teams or to me. And what a reflection on the student athletes and their coaches and the solid values of competition they were able to impart to their competitors.

In summarizing these accomplishments, I have deliberately avoided anecdotes about individual students, although I have hundreds of them. I once gave a speech at a civic meeting, sharing many wonderful stories of accomplishment and achievement by individual school system pupils. A critic in the audience that day objected to my presentation, saying that no number of individual success stories can speak to the group dynamics and culture of a school. There is some point to that, I suppose, so I have consciously avoided a thousand stories of individual shining stars. Instead, I have focused on the general culture of Upper Darby High School.

But for the record, at my home inside the school system boundaries, I often hosted student visitors much like the legendary Mr. Chips. I have also chatted with kids in stores and restaurants and on street corners. I regularly hosted students for breakfasts and luncheons at the administration building. In any given class at the high school, I knew names, serial numbers, and histories of hundreds of kids.

And it was always interesting to debrief students in college about how well their high school preparation had served them. I did a great deal of just that wandering around the stands during the traditional Thanksgiving football game, when many grads returned home from university for the holiday. As a result, I know from the viewpoints of Upper Darby High School students just who their best teachers were.

Much is being written these days about the importance of smaller schools, that larger schools are so often ineffective and impersonal. In a perfect world where money flowed for public education, I would have had double the number of schools that I did in my school district. But, that having been said, a dedicated and caring and loving school staff can overcome the barriers imposed by a large school facility and personalize it for the young people they serve.

15

MOTHER TERESA

During my more than thirty years of service in public education, I probably had substantial personal and in-depth professional contact with hundreds of school leadership figures—superintendents, central administrators, principals, and assistant principals as well school board members. Some I admired, and some I did not. But whatever the case, I was always an observer, looking for strengths and weaknesses, things that I might emulate or seek to avoid in my own leadership role.

Among all of those leadership figures, one stands highest in my mind. Teresa will always be identified in Upper Darby as the quintessential board president—forceful, in command, articulate, well-studied on the issues, and, most important, adamant in her advocacy of high-quality learning opportunities for the district's students.

At our monthly school board meetings, it was always easy to pick out the college students who were at these sessions on a class assignment—that is, to observe and write about a body of elected officials doing their business in public. After one board meeting, which had a little bit of everything in it, a young lady cornered me. She identified herself as a local university student and had taken thorough notes to which she now referred.

This college student was wide-eyed and excited. She was overwhelmed by what she had seen that night. Here was her question to me: "I have just watched the presiding board president at different times assuming the roles of a children's rights advocate, a military general, an accountant, a lawyer, a

CHAPTER 15

tax expert, a negotiator, a compromise agent, and, to top all of that, a gentle grandmother. Can you tell me which one of these she really is?" Spoken with all the sincerity and innocence of a nineteen-year-old on a quest.

"Truth be told, Teresa is all of these," I replied. "What you have just witnessed is the epitome of school leadership. Look as hard and as long as you want. You aren't going to find many in her class. For she is the very best at what she does."

Teresa's oratory and public eloquence were legendary. She delivered a prepared speech as well as anyone I have ever seen. But when she was extemporaneous, speaking to the matter at hand from her heart, she was truly awesome. Not someone you would want to get into a debate with because of her quickness of thought, Teresa also had that sense of timing that few have, the patience to wait and to gather her thoughts, and then, at just the right moment, to come out swinging! She used her God-given talents of pragmatism, intelligence, tact, foresight, daring, and compassion to cross a thousand bridges on behalf of her beliefs and principles. These are the marks of great leadership.

Teresa's life was about giving to others. She was a leader for all seasons. She most relished being amid pupils in school classrooms where she read books to the young and philosophized about government with the older students. They were the purpose for her life's work and they were ever in her heart.

Teresa loved chatting with teachers and principals. She was a listener and an empathizer, not some visiting expert. She was a fixture at hundreds of school events and especially enjoyed "gussying up" to accompany Joan and me to the annual senior proms. She was never too busy for a parent's concerns or an inquiry from some citizen on the street. She never ducked a reporter's question, and her candor was unrivaled. All of this created widespread admiration and respect from students, parents, teachers, administrators, board members, and other elected officials. So much so, that over the many years of her work, she came to be known throughout the school community as Upper Darby's own Mother Teresa.

In her later years she suffered with an illness that weakened her but never could crush her spirit. As she lay dying, the senior high concert choir came to the hospital to comfort her with the music she so loved. Amid a room filled with tearful young and old, Barbara, the district's music supervisor and

MOTHER TERESA

concert choir director, told Teresa that if her students could have only one wish granted, it would be for Teresa to be in attendance at the gala Christmas Concert only two months away. An inch from death, Teresa called upon all of the strength left in a life that was about to end. She told the Upper Darby choir members that one way or the other, she would be with them for this event. Teresa died shortly thereafter. And to this day I believe that she kept that promise. As a matter of fact, you can sense her presence throughout the Upper Darby School District even today.

The magnitude of the contributions of this great lady cannot be overstated. All of us are in the end what we have done, and what Teresa has done will live on forever.

Dearest Mother Teresa . . .

Rest comfortably now in peace for you have given so much to so many. For all who needed education, you were their relentless advocate. You gave the Upper Darby School District your tireless efforts throughout your life. You were our leader and you will never be forgotten.

For strength, you gave us your soul.

When indecisive, you gave us a shove.

For battles, you led us from the front.

When weary, you propped us up.

For purpose and direction, you shared your heart.

Whatever concerns arose, you always lent your ear.

For kindness, you opened your arms.

When all looked hopeless, you listened and cared.

And for all of our success, you never sought the limelight, just shared in our joy.

16

MY ODE TO THE UPPER DARBY SCHOOL COMMUNITY

How do I love thee? Let me count the ways.
I love thee to the depth and breadth and height
My soul can reach, when feeling out of sight
For the ends of Being and ideal Grace.
I love thee to the level of every day's
Most quite need, by sun and candlelight.

The borrowed words above echo in my brain whenever I reflect on my fourteen years as superintendent of schools in the Upper Darby School District. Those words are from Elizabeth Barrett Browning, who wrote those moving lines to express her affection and caring and concern for a loved one. Appropriately, her words are a superb expression of the love that I will always have for the school community that was my wonderful workplace and home for so many years.

Late in 1984, when I was named as superintendent of schools in Upper Darby, two incidents sent chills down my spine. The first episode was a telephone call from a superintendent in a nearby affluent, homogeneous school district. He wanted to wish me well, but he then issued an ominous prediction.

"The Upper Darby School District community is changing and not for the better," this superintendent pontificated. "People have begun to flee the city of Philadelphia. And your school system is going to end up with a great many of those inner-city kids. Added to that, your community is bound to

CHAPTER 16

suffer through racial unrest as neighborhoods experience this transition. If I were you, I would make a three-year plan to get out. What you've got is a great stepping stone to a superintendency somewhere else where you can succeed and live happily ever after."

I politely thanked my colleague for his well wishes. But what I really wanted to tell him was to go to hell. And then a local realtor added even more elitist icing to the cake. Joan and I were looking to move into the Upper Darby community. And this fool real estate agent spent most of his time predicting the demise of my new school district via its deteriorating demographics. He kept urging us to look for a home in a more upscale community. I short-circuited! My fuses blew! And when I threatened to go to his bosses and tell them that they had employed a moron to sell houses, the agent finally took his foot out of his mouth and did what he was supposed to do. Shortly thereafter, Joan and I purchased our new house inside the school district.

During the next fourteen years, the Upper Darby community did in fact change. It became much more heterogeneous. But there was no racial turmoil or neighborhood deterioration. The Upper Darby School District was a key to assimilating the many newcomers and to celebrating its cultural, racial, and ethnic diversity as a strength not a weakness. The district won many outside awards for its educational quality and innovations in curriculum and instruction, student services, and community outreach. We eliminated many weaknesses and built upon strengths. Throughout my superintendency, I was proud to call Upper Darby my home.

And so, with deepest respect for the poetess Browning, I sincerely apologize for this humble improvisation of her love poem by this Philly poet pretender:

How do I love thee, Upper Darby School Community? Let me count the ways:

I love you for not being a white-bread community. Your diversity, your unpretentious and nonmaterialistic nature, your solid values, and your sincere, hard-working, and caring citizenry have always given me inspiration and determination.

I love you for your trust in sending me thousands of your children. I have tried to prioritize each of them and inspire those who have worked for me to do the same.

MY ODE TO THE UPPER DARBY SCHOOL COMMUNITY

I love you for providing me with more than forty decent, giving, and dedicated school board members who challenged and inspired me and joined with me in a quest for education at its best.

I love you for your unwavering support of my teachers and principals and other staff in the education of your children.

I love you for the acceptance and affection you gave my wife and me as residents of the community. The hundreds of civic and school events we attended and were a part of will always be treasured memories for us.

I love you for your network of community services, from the Delaware County Hospital to the community Y to the senior citizen centers to the restaurants and banks and retail stores where I spent so much time checking your pulse.

I love you for the difficult local tax support you had to provide our schools when the Commonwealth of Pennsylvania had financially abandoned us.

I love you for the police and fire department personnel, who were by my side in so many times of need.

And I love you for the academic and personal miracles that were created for our young people because of our spirit of togetherness. It was a wonderful flight.

    Dearest Upper Darby, I love you freely as you strive for Right;
    I love thee purely, as you receive this Praise;
    I love you with a former superintendent's unwavering faith.
    With all of my breath, smiles, and tears for all my life!

EPILOGUE

Victor's is Philadelphia's restaurant for opera lovers. Located amid the dense rowhouses of South Philadelphia, it has a great tradition in Philly, often being a stopover spot for visiting world-class tenors and sopranos and featuring an unparalleled collection of original opera recordings.

On a spring evening, Joey and his wife, Joan, and their special guests sat amid Victor's patrons. Joey was resplendent in his black shirt and black leather sportcoat. Some patrons in the restaurant undoubtedly wondered whether Joey was a Catholic priest or a hit man. No one could have imagined that he was a school superintendent.

Joey had invited Barbara, the Upper Darby School District's superb supervisor of music, who had built a dynasty of music education in Upper Darby's schools, to bring some outstanding concert-quality performers from Upper Darby High to celebrate the completion of their senior years. Amanda was the latest of Barbara's never-ending streak of remarkable sopranos, a talented young lady headed for intense study of vocal performance in Italy and New York after graduation. The other student attendees were Nia, Craig, and Tim, all formidable vocalists themselves.

It was a joy-filled evening. As Joey's guests feasted on sumptuous pasta dishes, Victor's waiters and waitresses, who were mostly serious post-high school opera students, took turns entertaining the restaurant patrons. At appointed times, a bell would ring, which was the signal for silence. The piped-in recorded music would then accompany the designated waiter or waitress

EPILOGUE

as he or she sang some famous aria. And then the audience would erupt with applause and bravos and go back to eating until the next bell would ring.

Joey had requested that Amanda prepare a piece to sing at Victor's. However, he cautioned that he had no idea whether or not some unknown patron off the street would ever be allowed to perform during the crowded dinner hour. Joey was not being very honest about this.

There was much more going on that night at Victor's. For enjoying an order of homemade ravioli and a gallon of red wine at one special corner table were Sal, Rocco, and Guido. Joey had been telling his three old friends for months about the marvelous talent of Amanda as an opera singer. And so Sal, Rocco, and Guido were in attendance to check out Joey's appraisal. There was never any question that Amanda was going to get her chance to sing. It had all been arranged.

Sal, Rocco, Guido, and Joey had all become opera buffs in their older years. The funny thing about this was that in their early years of friendship back in the old neighborhood, they wouldn't have been caught dead listening to opera. During their boyhood, when the annual Italian festivals were held each summer and the streets where they lived were blocked off from cars, an orchestra had performed nightly concerts of opera music from a bandstand.

In those days, Joey and his buddies were much too busy having fun and getting into trouble to have bothered with listening to even one note of these opera concerts. And now, the four friends readily admitted to each other that among their fondest wishes would be to somehow relive and enjoy that available opera experience of their youth which they had all so deliberately ignored.

In the present, Victor's frequently helped the four friends make up for their lost youth. And now Amanda was going to add to that enjoyment. She was prepared to render Pergolesi's "Se tu m'ami, se tu sospiri" if given the chance. So when dinner was completed for Joey's guests, he summoned Victor's restaurant manager to the table.

Joey respectfully inquired: Could this youthful opera hopeful be given the chance to sing? Amanda was immediately questioned about her credentials and background as a vocalist and precisely what she wanted to sing and in what key. Finally, after thoughtful consideration, the manager gave his guarded approval. It was acting at its very best, worth at least an Emmy.

EPILOGUE

Within minutes, as Joey had known she would, Amanda was captivating the sophisticated Victor's crowd, singing with her heart out of the depths of her soul. She was in the zone, giving a performance of skill beyond her years that moved the audience and brought them to their feet at its conclusion. Sal, Rocco, and Guido were now among many restaurant patrons on their feet, cheering for this young soprano who had just had a life experience.

A few minutes later, Sal, Rocco, and Guido came to visit Joey's table. They of course ignored Joey, pretending not to know him, and focused on Amanda. "You have the voice of an angel," Sal told her. "It is a gift from God, so you must work hard in the future to be the very best singer you can be out of gratitude for this gift. I expect to read great things about you someday when you are performing at the Met. For now, young lady, remember my words. Work at perfection and it will be yours. C'ent anni!"

Sal, Rocco, and Guido bowed politely to Joey's guests and departed. Sal gave Joey an unseen wink. Life was still great fun. The four friends were still at it!

A SUMMARY OF THE MESSAGES OF THIS BOOK

The human fragility of any student is not to be underestimated. For how easy it is for a young person to become a nonentity. And how critically important it is for school staff members to intervene, to reach out with sensitivity to help a kid in trouble before she or he is lost forever.

Mentoring matters monumentally especially for the young people who need it the most. Empathy, support, motivation, and positive reinforcement from an adult who genuinely cares can change a life.

Quality teaching is certainly about opening the minds of students, but also their hearts and souls. It is about helping pupils struggle and grow through the trials of life inside and outside school. Teaching is not just a job. It is a vocation, a calling to make a difference for young people. Great teachers live this every day.

Communicating with the political power structure can be as vital to an educational system as communicating with parent constituents, a clergy roundtable, a civic organization, or a vested interest group.

Never be too quick to judge anyone or anything, especially on the basis of secondhand information or preconceived notions.

A SUMMARY OF THE MESSAGES OF THIS BOOK

The management of time is often what makes or breaks a school administrator.

Neither a construction manager nor an architect nor a clerk of the works can adequately deliver a project on time. Put your own gorillas in place for this purpose.

No compromise of integrity by a school leader is worth the potential consequences. And an ethics violation is seldom repairable.

The mission of the truly heroic educator is to push the youngster who is achieving well to even greater heights, to build achievement in that student who has been written off by others, to light some fire for the average, to give hope to that pupil who has no hope, to love the kid who has no love, and to always be a dream builder, not a dream breaker.

Many of public education's problems are outside the schools. As long as inadequate school funding and poverty prevail, as long as our government makes only minimal efforts to bridge the gaps between "haves and have-nots" educationally, the priority needs of American schooling will not be significantly addressed. Indeed, we have lost our way when testing has become the panacea for our nation's schools.

Because of the horrendous inadequacy of the press, government bureaucracies with political motivations, vested interest groups of all stripes, a host of empty-headed talking heads on the electronic media, biased think tanks and other ivory towers, and right-wingers have an unchallenged free rein to color the thinking of the American people regarding public education in any way they choose.

Given the sorry state of news media coverage of public education, coupled with the emergence of so many self-anointed, highly questionable experts on schooling in America, new and enhanced communication by people who know public schools best—teachers, school board members, support staff, and school administrators—has become a critical necessity.

A SUMMARY OF THE MESSAGES OF THIS BOOK

Creative thinking is forbidden in the Commonwealth of Pennsylvania.

A dedicated, caring, and loving school staff can overcome the barriers imposed by a large school facility and personalize it for the young people they serve.

Pragmatism, intelligence, tact, foresight, daring, and compassion ... these are the marks of great leadership.

BIBLIOGRAPHY

Altwerger, Bess. "Fight for the Right to Learn," *The Council Chronicle* (National Council of Teachers of English) 7, no. 5, Commentary Page.

Batory, Joseph P. *Yo! Joey!* (Lanham, MD: Scarecrow Press, 2002), 77–84.

Batory, Joseph P. "The Deteriorating Quality of News Media," *Spotlight* (Upper Darby, PA: Upper Darby School District) XXVIII, no. 2 (June 1997).

Berliner, David C., and Biddle, Bruce J. "The Lamentable Alliance between the Media and School Critics," *The School Administrator* 55, no. 8 (September 1998), 12–19.

Biddle, Bruce J. "Foolishness, Dangerous Nonsense, and Real Correlates of State Differences in Achievement," *Phi Delta Kappan* 79, no. 1 (September 1997), 8–13.

Bracey, Gerald W. "Summer Loss: The Phenomenon No One Wants to Deal With," and "More Trouble for Schools: The Volatility of Test Scores," *Phi Delta Kappan* 84, no. 1 (September 2002), 12–13.

Browning, Elizabeth Barrett. "Sonnets from the Portuguese, XLIII," in *How Do I Love Thee: The Love Letters of Robert Browning and Elizabeth Barrett* (New York: G.P. Putnam, 1969), 225.

Fitzwater, Ivan. *Effective Time Management* (San Antonio, TX: Management Development Institute, 1990).

Houston, Paul D. "Elevating Dreams to Reality," *The School Administrator* 59, no. 5 (May 2002), 46.

Kaplan, George R. *The Mass Media's Version of America's Schools.* (Washington, DC: Institute For Educational Leadership, 1992), 42.

BIBLIOGRAPHY

Logue, Timothy. "Board: Super Betrayed Trust," *Delaware County Daily Times*, January 26, 1999, p. 3.

Logue, Timothy. "School Boss Out in Spending Flap," *Delaware County Daily Times*, January 26, 1999, p. 3.

Purdy, Matthew. "After a Death, Talk Shifts from Official Ethics To Human Fairness," *The New York Times*, May 6, 2001, Metro Section, p. 1.

Steinberg, Laurence, B. Bradford Brown and Sanford M. Dornbusch. *Beyond The Classroom* (New York: Simon & Schuster, 1996), 18–20.

ABOUT THE AUTHOR

Joseph P. Batory was the superintendent of schools for the Upper Darby (PA) School District from 1984 through 1999. The school system serves a densely populated community that borders Philadelphia on its west side. Here is what people have said about his career:

"It is my pleasure to recognize and honor Joe Batory with the American Association of School Administrator's Distinguished Lifetime Service Award for his exemplary achievements in education and administration throughout his career."
—Paul Houston, Executive Director, American Association of School Administrators

"Joe Batory's tenure as superintendent has been exemplary and of the highest quality."

—Joseph Oravitz, Executive Director, Pennsylvania School Boards Association

"Joe Batory will always be a winner in the Upper Darby community and a friend to public school educators everywhere."
—Robert Dambman, President, Upper Darby Educators' Association

ABOUT THE AUTHOR

"A champion for the rights of school children everywhere. Joe Batory is courageous, credible, and caring!"
—Public Tribute, Upper Darby School Administrators Association

"After an exhaustive examination of his credentials and career accomplishments by an independent jury of prestigious educational leaders, Joe Batory has been singled out as one of the Top 100 practicing school administrators in North America."
—IBM Educational Systems and *Executive Educator* Magazine

JOEY LETS IT ALL HANG OUT!

Reflections of an Award-Winning School Superintendent

JOSEPH P. BATORY

A SCARECROWEDUCATION BOOK

The Scarecrow Press, Inc.
Lanham, Maryland, and Oxford
2003

A SCARECROWEDUCATION BOOK

Published in the United States of America
by Scarecrow Press, Inc.
A Member of the Rowman & Littlefield Publishing Group
4501 Forbes Boulevard, Suite 200, Lanham, Maryland 20706
www.scarecroweducation.com

PO Box 317
Oxford
OX2 9RU, UK

Copyright © 2003 by Joseph P. Batory

All rights reserved. No part of this publication may be reproduced, stored in a retrieval system, or transmitted in any form or by any means, electronic, mechanical, photocopying, recording, or otherwise, without the prior permission of the publisher.

British Library Cataloguing in Publication Information Available

Library of Congress Cataloging-in-Publication Data

Batory, Joseph P. (Joseph Patrick)
   Joey lets it all hang out! : reflections of an award-winning school superintendent / Joseph P. Batory.
      p. cm.
   "A ScarecrowEducation book."
   Includes bibliographical references (p.   ).
   ISBN 0-8108-4718-3 (pbk. : alk. paper)
   1. School superintendents—United States. 2. Educational leadership—United States. I. Title.
LB2831.72.B38 2003
371.2'011—dc21

                                                      2002155198

∞™ The paper used in this publication meets the minimum requirements of American National Standard for Information Sciences—Permanence of Paper for Printed Library Materials, ANSI/NISO Z39.48-1992.
Manufactured in the United States of America.

LB2831.72 .B38 2003
Batory, Joseph P. (Joseph Patrick)
Joey lets it all hang out! : reflections of an award-winning school superintendent